Botanical Ecstasies

Psychoactive Plant Formulas in India and Beyond

Matthew Clark

First published by
Psychedelic Press
London, United Kingdom

ISBN: 9781916266711

www.psychedelicpress.co.uk

Psychedelic Press
Independent Book Publisher

Contents

Acknowledgements

Many thanks to Robert Dickins, Nikki Wyrd, Peter Sjöstedt-Hughes and all at Psychedelic Press for graciously facilitating the publishing of this book.

Matthew Clark, Hove (UK), April 2021

PREFACE

For around 250 years, scholars have debated the botanical identity of *soma/haoma*, a plant potion that features in the *Veda*s, the sacred texts of the Brahmans of India, and in the *Avesta*, the sacred texts of Zoroastrians. *Soma/haoma* is reputed to have qualities both medicinal and mystical. Through examination of the relevant texts and by considering what we know of plant species native to Asia, in this monograph some proposals are made as to the likely ingredients of this potion, what its effects were, and furthermore, the influence these effects may have had on the development of religious experience in the Old World.

The thesis, first published in 1968, of R. Gordon Wasson, the banker-turned-scholar and pioneer of ethnomycology, proposed that *soma*, the ancient ritual drink of South Asia—the so-called 'nectar of immortality'—was the red, spotted fly-agaric mushroom (*Amanita muscaria*). Wasson was the first to put forward an argument that in ancient Asia a psychedelic plant, in this instance a fungus, was used in religious rituals. Even though his fly-agaric proposition has been challenged by many commentators, Wasson's claim that *soma* had a psychedelic/entheogenic effect has nevertheless been widely credited. Much more is now known about the effects of psychedelic compounds than was known half a century ago, and it now seems timely to return to the discussion of the possible use of psychedelics in ancient Asian ritual, but this time equipped with a broader understanding of the use and effects of such compounds.

In this monograph I endorse the proposal that the ancient Asian ritual drink known as *soma/haoma* was a concoction that could engender psychedelic/entheogenic effects; not all scholars accept this notion. This concoction was, I suggest, a multi-plant formula that would have varied depending on the local availability of psychoactive plants. It is proposed that one of the keys to the entheogenic efficacy of multi-plant formulas used in ancient Asia lies in the chemistry of ayahuasca; some ayahuasca analogues are explored. It also seems probable that substantive human experiences of non-ordinary states of consciousness would have initially been accidentally induced by plants. Yogic practices may have developed subsequently as a way of attaining non-ordinary states of consciousness without the use of psychoactive plants.

1. INTRODUCTION

In several articles[1] and a monograph (Clark 2020 [2017])[2] I have argued that the ancient Asian ritual drink known as *soma* to South Asian Brahmans and as *haoma* to Zoroastrians,[3] the so-called 'nectar of immortality',[4] was never based on a single plant, as hitherto sought by nearly all researchers. Instead, I propose that *soma* was generally the name for the juices expressed from at least two plants and from several

1. Clark (2015; 2018a; 2019a; 2019b; 2019c).

2. Some of the material presented in this article has previously appeared in the publications referred to above. Detailed below are recent observations and discoveries that have emerged during the course of research since the first publication of my monograph on this topic in 2017.

3. The common, late-Bronze Age source of the Zoroastrian *haoma* and Vedic *soma* cults, reflected in mythical tropes and ritual procedures, was first articulated in the mid-nineteenth century (Houben 2003:2.1). Comparisons between elements of the two cults were provided over a century ago by Macdonell (1995:113–114). See also: Eggeling (1885:xi–xxxii [*Satapatha Brāhmaṇa*, vol. 2 = *SBE* vol. 26]); Modi (1922:299–300). Further detailed work on this topic has been published more recently by Sadovski (e.g. Sadovski 2018). The two central elements of ancient Zoroastrianism and Vedic religion were the cults of the ritual fire(s) and the *soma/haoma* concoction (Bowman 1970:7; Boyce 1975:176; Malandra 1983:150; Watkins 1978:13). See Jurewicz (2010:191–195) for the Vedic, mythological homologies between *soma*/Soma and Agni (fire); and how they both function as transformers of reality.

4. It is apparent that the use of *soma/haoma* was wider than the cults of Brahmans and Zoroastrians. A branch of the fierce, horse-riding Scythians (Saka/Sakā/Śāka), who roamed Asia from southern Russia to eastern China between about the 9th century BCE until 4th century CE, were known as *haomavarga* (*haoma* twisters) (Abaev 1975:2; Bartholomae 1904:1735; Gershevitsch 1974:4–5). In an inscription of Darius (who fought the Scythians), several kinds of Saka are mentioned, including *haomavarga* and *tigrazanda* (pointed-hat) (Koryakova and Epimachov 2014:225; Parpola 2015:102). (Scythians also used and cultivated cannabis for cloth and inebriation: Herodotus 1968:265–266.) *Haoma* was also used in the cult of Mithras, which from the latter part of the 1st millennium BCE until the early centuries CE stretched from north Africa to Scotland, and was almost as widespread as Christianity. The cult was particularly popular with soldiers. Bowman (1970) examines a body of Aramaic inscriptions on mortars and pestles, mostly made of green chert, and plates found in Persepolis (in Iran), dated to the 5th century BCE, many inscribed during the reign of Artaxerxes (r.465–425 BCE. *Haoma* was drunk at Mithraic festivals and was used at Persepolis in the Achaemenid period from at least the time of Xerxes (r.486–365) (Bedrosian 2000; Bowman 1970:8ff.). It has been argued that the Achaemenians were in fact mostly Zoroastrian (Antia 2006). It is also proposed (Clark 2020) that a concoction similar to *soma/haoma* was the *kykeōn* (mixed potion) drunk during Greek mystery rites.

other additive plants;[5] the formula for *soma/haoma* would have varied, comprising different ingredients, depending on geographical location and the availability of local plants. I also argue, based on the available evidence provided in Brahmanical and Zoroastrian texts, that *soma/haoma* was a psychedelic/entheogenic concoction,[6] with similar but not identical effects to those of the 'classic' tryptamine alkaloids, LSD and psilocybin, which have a particular and distinct capacity for inducing 'classic' mystical experiences.[7] *Soma/haoma* was also, like ayahuasca (see below), a purgative: it could induce vomiting.[8]

In both the *Veda*s and the *Avesta*, *soma/haoma* is identified as a deity,[9] as a plant and as the pressed extrusion of plants.[10] The linguistic root of the term *soma/haoma* is √*su* (Sanskrit)/√*hu* (Avestan), which refers to a juice expressed or squeezed out—through (usually) pounding with stones in Vedic rituals, or using mortar and pestle in Zoroastrian

5. In Vedic and Zoroastrian texts, '*soma/haoma*' may refer to the expressed juice of plants, or to the plant/plants themselves, or to the god Soma/Haoma.

6. This is disputed particularly by some proponents of the 'ephedra thesis' (see below). Effects from *soma*—which include sensations of flying, seeing light, becoming poetically inspired, feeling 'immortal', and undergoing an ordeal or a (terrifying) near-death experience and consequent 'rebirth'—may be discerned from several, oft-cited Vedic passages (*ṚV* 10.119 [*Labasūkta* 'song of the lapwing']; 8.48.3–4; 9.54.3; 9.64.4; 9.107.20; 9.113.9). For intimations in the *Avesta* of the effects of *haoma*, see *Hōm Yašt* 9–11. For a wider, more detailed assessment of the effects of *soma/haoma*, see Clark (2020:49–59).

7. Perrine (1996:258) details the broad similarity of effects of these three substances. There are of course distinct variables in the range of experiences engendered by these compounds but also a distinct core of similarities (see Griffiths *et al.* 2019).

8. *Taittirīya Saṃhitā* (of the *Yajurveda*) 2.3.2.6; Śatapatha Brāhmaṇa 5.5.4.8–13; 12.7.2.1–2; 12.7.3.9–10.

9. In the *Puraṇa*s *soma*/Soma features as both the beverage and deity (homologized with the Moon-god and also occasionally identified or associated with Kubera), with a fully-developed mythological biography; see, for example, *Vāyu Purāṇa* (II. 1.135; II. 2.30–48); *Agni Purāṇa* (56.27); and also occasionally as a king (of plants), for example, *Agni Purāṇa* (18.25); and even homologized, together with Agni, as the tubular organs that end at the nostrils (*Agni Purāṇa* 30.33). Soma, as an incarnation of Brahmā, is born as one of the three sons of Anasūyā (*Mārkaṇḍeya Purāṇa* 17.4–11). Soma rejuvenates living beings and is one of the eight Vasus (nature deities); Śiva (as Soma) is the soul of time (*kālātman*) and 'perfect' knowledge (*vijñāna*) (*Liṅga Purāṇa* 34.3; 58.20a; 86.94).

10. See Macdonell (1995:104–115) for references in the *Veda*s.

ritual[11]—and does not refer to a specific plant or plants. Given that *soma/haoma* is capable of producing psychedelic/entheogenic effects—appearing to have the potential to propel the consumer through an epistemic barrier into another dimension of consciousness—*soma/haoma* could, I suggest, be loosely translated as 'psychedelic' or 'entheogenic'.[12] Furthermore, as with any psychedelic, such compounds may be used at lower dose-levels to provide remedial treatment for various psychological, physiological or mental conditions.[13] There is some evidence for this kind of use in ancient South Asia (see below).

The evidence in the *Avesta* and the *Veda*s, the composition of which dates to between *c.*1600 and 700 BCE, indicates that *soma/haoma* preparations of ancient Asia produced potentially psychedelic effects. However, for many centuries the Brahmans of South Asia, on the rare occasions when they perform *soma* rituals[14] (which are the most important and esteemed Vedic rituals),[15] they have used substitute plants—usually the vine-like *Sarcostemma bevistigma/acidum* or *Periploca aphylla*[16]—which exude a milky sap and are called *soma* but have no psychoactive effect; and the Brahmans know that these are

11. See Clark (2020:10–16) for Vedic practices; and pp. 25–34 for *haoma* in the *Avesta.*

12. Also suggested by Müller-Ebeling *et. al* (2002:178).

13. Although scientific studies of the effects of micro- and low-dose psychedelics began in the late 1940s in Switzerland, it is only in the last ten years or so that the potential benefits of such use for depression, trauma, creativity and other conditions have been more widely studied and evaluated (see Passie 2019). See Schroder (2014) for a collection of personal testimonies that recount the therapeutic benefits of LSD and MDMA. See Stolaroff (1994) for accounts of psycho-therapeutic experiences produced by a range of novel, psychedelic chemicals.

14. See Smith (2001) for an account of recently performed *soma* rituals in the state of Maharashtra.

15. There are around 160 Vedic *śrauta* rituals, see Dandekar (1958–1962). See Knipe (2015) for an account of a community of Brahmans in Andhra Pradesh, for whom *soma* rituals are preeminent.

16. See Houben 2003:2.4); Gupta (2013:71); O'Flaherty (1969:119–121). *Sacostemma brevistigma/Asclepias acida* is still currently used in *soma* rites in costal Andhra Pradesh (Knipe 2015:213).

'substitutes'.[17] Zoroastrians in both Iran and India (the Parsees) use—or previously used—the ephedra plant (see below), which has a mild stimulant effect.[18] However, small-scale use of psychedelic *haoma* concoctions persists in Iran, where Qalandar Sūfīs[19] prepare ayahuasca-analogue concoctions (Clark 2020:34–35),[20] and in Bengal where some Tāntrikas also manufacture *soma* (see Section 11).

17. The issue of substitute/alternative *soma* plants is treated extensively in Clark (2020:ch. 4). Many of these plants appear to be grasses of different kinds, some of which may possibly be psychoactive. Around a dozen substitute plants are recorded in the *Brāhmaṇas* (which date from *c.*800 BCE); see Kane (1997, vol. 2, part 2,:1203); Kuiper (1984:219–220); Swamy (1976:16–18).

18. Zoroastrians in Yazd, Iran use ephedra as *haoma* (O'Flaherty 1969:118, 122); the Parsis of Mumbai used to import ephedra stalks until several decades ago (Modi 1922).

19. These are radical Sūfīs who neither pray nor read the *Koran*; they live *be-shār* (outside the law) and consume *bhāṅg* (cannabis) to excess. See Clark (2016); Digby (1984); Karamustafa (2006); Tortel (2009) for further details.

20.This report is based on (I believe, fully reliable) information from a single informant, who is a scholar of Persian and Arabic and a fully experienced *ayahuascero*. He participated in a ceremony in northern Iran conducted by Qalandar Sūfīs on condition that he ask no questions. The experience was similar to that of strong ayahuasca. The only clue to the possible ingredients of the *haoma* were many Syrian rue plants (*Pegamon harmala*) growing around the temple where the ritual was performed.

2. YOGIC PRACTICES AND ENDOGENOUS *SOMA*

Research has demonstrated that many animals, including insects, birds and mammals, naturally inebriate themselves, when given the opportunity, with various plants and fermented juices. They may test substances for inebriation potential; if there is an effect, creatures will often tend to repeatedly use those substances (Samorini 2002; Siegal 2005). Baker (2009:394) suggests that the human discovery of psychoactive plants, fungi, minerals, and even animals, may have served as the catalysts that would eventually lead to other techniques for voluntarily altering consciousness. Experiences derived from attempts to modify or alter consciousness through yogic practices or austerities (*tapas*) of one kind or another, in an attempt to attain non-ordinary states of consciousness without the use of psychoactive plants, would, I suggest, logically have been subsequent to plant-engendered experiences.[21] In the light of this likelihood, it is therefore relevant to attempt to identify the plants that could have been used in ancient ritual environments for potentially entheogenic or psychedelic experience and to evaluate the parameters of their effects.

If the conclusions of this research are valid and if, by the middle of the second millennium BCE, experiences of plant-based enlightenment[22] were indeed embedded in South Asian culture—certainly in the

21. Similarly, in the 1960s and 1970s, experience with psychedelics—particularly LSD—influenced many people in the USA to take up Buddhist meditation practices (Osto 2019).

22. For discussions and analysis of plant- or chemical-based mysticism and whether or not this is in any way different from mystical experience arising spontaneously or engendered by other techniques, see Griffiths *et al.* (2019); Hendricks (2018); Hood Jr. (2014): drug-induced and

Brahmanical world and probably wider—it could be argued that this proposition has a significant bearing when it comes to evaluating the history of yoga practices, Indian philosophy in general, and the western, esoteric understanding of South Asian history.

Yogic practices, such as meditation and *prāṇāyāma*, could be understood as originally attempts to engender trance states without the use of psychoactive plants. It is well known that the primary emic aim of the study and comprehension of any of the classic Brahmanical systems (*darśana*s) of Indian philosophy is to attain liberation (*mokṣa*) or enlightenment. With plant-based experiences of a theistic or of a non-dual reality in the cultural background, such philosophical pursuits are perhaps better comprehended. It could also be noted that the use of *soma/haoma* was only ever for the elite, a very small percentage of the general population. The formulas for entheogenic concoctions have remained practically unknown until very recently, and are still largely obscure. The Brahmans charged exorbitant fees for participation in *soma* rituals;[23] they would not have wished readily to divulge the

non-drug-induced mystical experiences are remarkably similar. See also Griffiths *et al.* (2006; 2011) for assessments of mystical experiences induced through psilocybin in controlled laboratory conditions. See Hobson (2001) for how the neurophysiological basis of all kinds of altered states of consciousness—including dreaming, hypnosis, psychosis and psychedelic experience—is fundamentally the same, and depends on the activity of specific neurotransmitter mechanisms; a similar view is argued for by Hulin (2014:191n.1) and Winkelman (2014). See Clark (1969) and Houston and Masters (2000) [1966] for what are now 'classic' assessments of psychedelic drug-induced mystical experiences. Hanegraaf (2014) contends that after the criminalization of psychedelics in the 1960s, several 'new age' reports of mystical experience in the 1980s and 1990s were actually drug-induced, but not reported to be thus derived at the time. Horgan (2004) interviews around a dozen prominent American writers on mysticism, who have a variety of perspectives: psychedelic-induced mystical experience can no longer be dismissed as 'merely' drug-induced. See Bache (2019) for a personal account and explanation of a range of profound, 'classic' mystical experiences induced by LSD. Ott (1997a) argues comprehensively for the primacy of entheogens-based mysticism over what he describes as the artificial mysticism of religious practice, the latter being (p. 16) "inferior forms of mysticism" using merely "placebo" sacraments (Ott 1995:13ff.). See also Clark (2020:77–102) for further discussion and references.

23. Based on data provided by various ethnographies, it can be roughly estimated that Brahmans comprise (both now and probably historically) only about 4% of India's population; and not all Brahmans would have drunk *soma*. An invited participant might only drink *soma* once in a

'secrets' of their concoctions, which would have required expertise in the botany of psychoactive plants, and which, if prepared incorrectly, could have resulted in a very unpleasant experience or even death.

Although it is argued that *soma/haoma* was originally a psychoactive plant concoction, used for many centuries in religious rituals, it is also apparent that *soma*, in the South Asian context particularly, became homologized with both a mythological nectar of immortality (*amṛta*), which features in the epics and in the *Purāṇa*s, and also with an internal nectar, stored in the head, which can be accessed through yogic practice.

Soma is identified with the Sun in earlier Vedic passages, while in later Vedic texts *soma* is more commonly identified with the Moon.[24] Another of the many epithets and synonyms of *soma* in the *Veda*s is *amṛta* (non-death/immortality); the drinking of *soma* can lead to immortality.[25] However, the well-known South Asian myth of the 'churning of the ocean of milk' (*kṣīrābhdimanthana*), from which the *rasāmṛta/somarasa* (the precious juice/nectar of immortality) emerges, appears only later, unexpectedly and in highly developed form (Long 1976:177) in the *Rāmāyaṇa* and *Mahābhārata* (*c.*200 BCE–200 CE) and *Purāṇa*s (*c.*300–1200 CE).[26]

lifetime, owing to the cost. *Manusmṛti* (XI.7–8) states: "A man who has sufficient resources to maintain his dependents for three years, or someone who has more than that, is entitled to drink Soma. If a twice-born man who possesses fewer resources than that drinks Soma, he will not reap its reward, even though he may never have drunk Soma before" (trans. Olivelle). *Viṣṇusmṛti* (59.8–9) says that someone with a sufficient supply of food should perform the *soma* sacrifice once a year, in spring. Similarly, in Iran, in the cult of Mithra in the early centuries BCE, the majority of participants drank *haoma* only once but some participated several times (Bowman 1970:35). Outside Asia, the historical use of psychedelics appears similarly to have been limited to relatively small sections of native populations, and was nothing like as popular or widespread, nor necessarily used for 'spiritual' purposes, as some modern enthusiasts would like to believe (Singh 2020).

24. See Clark (2020:18n.61) for references.

25. *ṚV* 6.44.16; 6.44.23; 8.48.3; 9.91.2; 9.110.4. The sacrificer becomes immortal by drinking *soma* (*ŚB* 3.3.3.10).

26. See, for example, *Bhāgavata Purāṇa* 8.6.33–8.7. For the details of the myth, see Clark (2018b).

The concept of *amṛta* is particularly significant, because in trance states, whether induced through psychoactive plants or yogic practice, the person experiences a timeless state, which is a fundamental hallmark of mystical states (for example, Zaehner 1972:7), in which there is no death, as there is no time.

Identified as the Moon—and usually paired with the Sun—*soma* as *amṛta* appears in Tantric and subsequently in yoga texts as an internal nectar stored in the cranial vault.[27] Through Tantric ritual or yoga practice, access to this internal nectar is said to provide an experience of liberating ecstasy. Thus, it can be seen how the notion of *amṛta* transitioned from referring to an experience engendered through psychoactive plants to a concept of an internal, liberating nectar that can be accessed through yoga, without the use of these plants.

27. See, for example, the 15th-century *Haṭhapradīpikā* (3.44–46): describing the *khecarī mudrā* (a yogic practice of placing the curled-back, extended tongue over the top of the palate), it is stated that, "The knower of yoga—tongue above, steady, drinking soma—undoubtedly conquers death in half a month. Poison does not spread in the yogi whose body is filled every day with drops of soma—even when bitten by the Takshaka serpent. As the fire, the fuel, and the flame, the oily wick, so the soul does not abandon the body filled with drops of soma" (trans. Akers). Similarly, in the *c.*14th-century *Khecarīvidyā* of Ādināth (2.16–36), *soma* is identified as an internal nectar (*amṛta*)—stored in eight places (*kalā*), or as eight streams/oceans—in one's head, 'drinking' which, through *khecarī mudrā*, the yogi conquers disease and acquires a diamond body (trans. Mallinson 2007:124). Also, in the Tamil *siddha* tradition it is believed that there is an endogenous *soma* (correlative with exogenous *soma*), which is a fluid known as *civampu* (the flowering of *civam*) that is secreted by the midbrain, and which can be activated by yoga exercises (Zvelebil 1996:92).

3. THE BOTANICAL CANDIDATES FOR *SOMA/HAOMA*

In the publications referred to above in the Introduction, I present more detailed arguments as to why not one of the several dozen botanical candidates for *soma/haoma* that has so far been proposed in the last 250 years, since scholarly speculation first began, is apt;[28] they either do not fit textual descriptions of the form of *soma/haoma* or do not have a suitable, psychedelic/entheogenic effect. Many of the plant candidates that have been proposed are, I argue, psychoactively too weak *on their own* to produce properly entheogenic effects,[29] while others are too toxic.[30] This does not rule out the likelihood that many of the weaker psychoactive plants that have been proposed may have been consumed together with other, more strongly psychoactive plants in multiple-plant formulas, which is a general proposition being advanced in this monograph (see below).

The three botanical candidates that still have some academic support are Syrian/mountain rue (*Peganum harmala*), the fly-agaric mushroom (*Amanita muscaria*), and various kinds of ephedra.[31]

There is evidence of the use of Syrian rue by humans dating from *c.*4000 BCE in the Caucasus region, and later in Mesopotamia and Egypt

28. See Clark (2020) for a treatment of numerous botanical candidates. For a summary, see Clark (2019:106–107). See Samorini (2017) for a bibliography of publications on *soma/haoma*. The most comprehensive surveys of botanical candidates are by [Doniger] O'Flaherty (1969) and Houben (2003).

29. These include water-lily (*Nymphaea caerulea*), ginseng and cannabis.

30. These include mandrake, varieties of datura and the ergot fungus.

31. See Clark (2020) for a discussion of these plants and their effects.

(Samorini 2018:165–167; 2019a). However, in brief, Syrian rue on its own is not properly entheogenic/psychedelic, except in high doses when it additionally becomes toxic, unpleasant and destabilizing; it is more accurately an 'oneirophrenic', being dream-inducing and producing a passive, introverted state.[32] It has a long history of use as a medicine,[33] a 'visionary' plant and an aphrodisiac. Known as *isphand/isfand/spand/sipand* [34] throughout the Middle-East and Asia (and *harmal* in Arabic), it was first proposed as *soma* by the great orientalist William Jones in 1794.[35]

Syrian rue contains the β-carbolines harmine, harmaline and tetrahydroharmine, which act as MAOIs, thus potentiating DMT (see below). It has been proposed by some commentators that rue may have been combined with the ephedra plant (see below) in a psychoactive concoction. However, this seems improbable, because adverse reactions may occur with this combination.[36]

The red and white-spotted fly-agaric mushroom was famously first proposed to be *soma* by R. Gordon Wasson, one of the great pioneers

32. See Naranjo (1973), who conducted pioneering research in 1963 on the effects of harmine and harmaline, which, together with tetrahydroharmine, are β-carboline derivatives and are the main active ingredient chemicals of Syrian rue and also of the *Banisteriopsis caapi* vine.

33. It is discussed by the medical authorities Pliny (*Natural History* 20.51) and Dioscorides (3.51–54) (2000:423–428); one of its names was *moly.*

34. In Egypt it was known as the 'Bes' plant (named after a deity).

35. Flattery and Schwarz (1989) provide an extensive treatment of the history of use of Syrian rue/*harmal*; for reports of the effects of rue, see Beyer (2010:215); DeKorne (2011:146); Jay (1999:85ff.); Ott (1994:45); Samorini (2019a); Stolaroff (2004:86). See also Samorini (2019b:232–246) on the discovery and potential of β-carbolines and MAOIs.

36. Schwarz (2006:222) suggests that the 'visionary' plant rue was pounded together with ephedra, adding a stimulant component. Pendell (2010:129) warns against using ephedra with an MAOI; he notes that combining ephedrine with moclobemide, a reversible MAO-A inhibitor, was found to potentiate four-fold ephedrine's effect on blood pressure, and an 0.6 increase in heart-rate. The most common adverse reactions were palpitations and headache. Nevertheless, ephedrine can potentiate DMT and other psychedelics (DeKorne *et al.* 2002:25). Robinson (1968:132) comments that ephedrine inhibits MAO activity *in vitro.* Gracie and Zarkof (1991:no. 10, 'An Indo-European Plant Teacher' p. 4) warn against combining an MAO with ephedrine: it could be fatal.

of ethnomycology, in *Soma: Divine Mushroom of Immortality*, initially published in 1968; this was followed by a series of articles, up until 1986.[37] Apart from ayahuasca analogues, fly-agaric is one of the very few—and certainly most influential—psychedelic plants that has so far been proposed for *soma/haoma*.[38] However, contrary to Wasson's thesis, fly-agaric mushrooms do not, as described in Vedic and Zoroastrian texts, require pounding in a mortar and pestle or with stones to extract juice. In Siberia they are usually natively consumed either whole, peeled or dried; though in the Shutul Valley in Afghanistan there is a preparation made from the dried powder (Piper 2019:137).[39] The mushrooms do not come in the form of bundles of stalks (as described in Vedic and Zoroastrian texts); the use of any kind of mushroom is strictly prohibited in Brahmanical legal texts (*Dharmaśāstra*);[40] and the effects on most consumers is usually quite destabilizing, causing blurred vision and stomach cramps.[41] There are, however, also positive

37. Among other extant supporters of the fly-agaric thesis are Stuhrman (1985; 2006) and Levitt (2011).

38. Di Maio (2013) has found the San Pedro cactus *Echinopsis pachanoi* (or a very close relative), which contains mescaline, growing in Himachal Pradesh in India, and proposes this as *soma*. However, no cactus species is historically native to anywhere outside the Americas (Rojas-Aréchiga and Flores 2016:21–25). Schroeder and Guzmán (1981) propose psilocybin mushrooms (found growing in Nepal); but see below on the improbability of any mushroom being *soma*. A few websites (e.g. *Entheology.org* 2020) host discussions of Hawaiian baby woodrose as a possible candidate for *soma*. This plant is used by some shamans in Nepal and is also suggested as a *soma* plant by Müller-Ebeling *et al.* (2002:167). The seeds of this vine-like plant (*Argyreia nervosa*, Sanskrit *vidhārā/adhoguḍa*), contain lysergic acid amide (LSA, or ergine)—also contained in the seeds of several morning glory species (also in the *Convolvulaceae* family)—which is precursor for the manufacture of LSD. A close relative of *Argyreia nervosa* is *Argyreia speciosa* (elephant creeper/woolly morning glory; Sanskrit *bastāntrī/chagalāntrikā/vṛdhadāra/vṛdhadārakal/vṛdhadāra*; Hindi *samundar ka pat/samundarsokha*), which is also native to South Asia and has uses in Āyurveda. LSA can have psychedelic effects. It is probably one of the plants that was used in *soma* concoctions: see below and Clark (2020:187–188n.605) for further details.

39. Feeney (2010) demonstrates that drying the mushrooms prior to consumption significantly reduces their toxicity.

40. See Falk (2002/3:146); Padhy and Dash (1997); *Manusmṛti* 5.5, 5.19, 6.14, 11.156.

41. This was the effect on McKenna (1992:109).

reports.[42] Wasson consumed fly-agaric mushrooms several times in 1965 and 1966 but only felt either nauseous or fatigued (Wasson 1969:75). He derived no mystical experience from taking fly-agaric, unlike the revelations he derived from ingesting psilocybin mushrooms: first in Mexico in 1955 and subsequently in New York.[43]

Even though Wasson was almost certainly wrong about *soma* being the fly-agaric mushroom, he is widely credited with introducing the notion that *soma* was psychedelic/entheogenic.[44] Wendy Doniger, who worked with Wasson on his *Soma* book, translated Sanskrit passages for

42. Heinrich (1995:191–198; 2014:291–297) on one occasion, after eating fly-agaric, experienced the white light of the Godhead; there are reports of Siberians who can perform great feats of walking, hunting or singing after eating the mushrooms (Furst 1988:38, 51–59; Saar 1991); it is used for shamanic rites by Ostyak and Vogul tribes in western Siberia, and by Kamchadal, Koryak and Chukchi tribes in eastern Siberia (Piper 2019:135); fly-agaric mushrooms are also used for initiation and divination among the Ojibway tribe, whose homeland straddles Canada and the USA (Navet 1988).

43. Despite the objections to the *soma*/fly-agaric mushroom thesis that have been articulated by numerous scholars since Wasson's first publication in 1968—see Smith (1972) for a survey of both supporters and opponents of Wasson's thesis—the fly-agaric proposition has been so influential that researchers have found supposed evidence of historical fly-agaric use in religious practices in ancient Egypt (Puharich 1959); early Christianity (Allegro 1973 [1970]; Heinrich 1995; Irvin and Rutajit 2009; Rush 2011; Klapp 2013; Brown and Brown 2016), South Asia (Maillart-Garg and Winkelman 2019), Buddhism (Hajicek-Dobberstein 1995; Crowley 2016) and Greek religion (Wohlberg 1990; Ruck 2006; Ruck *et al.* 2011).

Ott (1997a:133n.72) notes that Puharich met Wasson in the mid-1950s and that Allegro was also clearly inspired by Wasson's thesis. Neither Puharich's nor Allegro's research was ever endorsed by serious scholars. Hatsis (2016) argues against Brown and Brown (2016); Letcher (2007:141–152) summarizes and critiques the findings of Wasson, Hajicek-Dobberstein, Ruck, and other fly-agaric enthusiasts. Some commentators maintain that such was the secrecy of mushroom use in South Asia that there is no specific word for 'mushroom' in Sanskrit. This is incorrect: in the *Ṛgveda* (1.84.8) the term *kṣumpa* is used, albeit once, for 'mushroom' (Bailey 1984; Dandekar 1994:22); the term persists in Hindi as *khumbhī.*

Dannaway (2009) goes further in proposing fly-agaric as the pan-Asian *soma*. Wasson's additional supposition (1969:81–85) that the 'supernatural plant' in pre-Buddhist China was fly-agaric is based on an erroneous translation of *tche* (which has twigs and leaves) in Chinese texts (Demiéville 1970). Even though fly-agaric grows in South Asia—in Jammu and Kashmir, around Manali (in Himachal Pradesh), in Kodaikanal (in Tamil Nadu), and in Guntur (in Andhra Pradesh, though maybe introduced here by Europeans), see Rawala *et al.* (2002:34); and also in Nepal (Müller-Ebeling *et al.* (2002:176)—if the totality of the available evidence concerning *soma* is properly considered, then, I suggest, the fly-agaric thesis, initially popularized by Wasson, is perhaps one of the largest red herrings (or red mushrooms!) ever introduced into religious studies. The notion, even taught in schools in Sweden, that the Norse berserkers ate fly-agaric, has also recently been challenged: there is no evidence for this; they may instead have intoxicated themselves with henbane (Fatur 2019).

44. Staal 2001:762–763; Ott 1998:33; Houben 2003:3.1.

him, and contributed a substantial section on botanical identifications, was always sceptical of his thesis.[45] However, she comments (1997:58) that his discovery of the psychedelic/entheogenic properties of *soma* is not only important in itself but also "casts an entirely new light on the whole of Indian religious history, particularly on esoteric traditions and on yoga techniques".

The ephedra plant has for several decades been the botanical candidate for *soma/haoma* most widely endorsed by scholars, particularly by Zoroastrian specialists.[46] However, juice extracted from the stalks of the ephedra bush (the ephedrine content of which varies, depending on species),[47] acts as a stimulant similar to caffeine or adrenaline.[48] This plant is widely distributed in Asia,[49] is well known in

45. Fifty years ago, Wasson submitted to the *Bulletin of the School of Oriental and African Studies* a rejoinder to opponents—primarily the Sanskritist John Brough—defending his already-published thesis (1968) that *soma* was the fly-agaric mushroom. The article was rejected by the editors of the *Bulletin.* Wasson had his article instead published by the Botanical Museum of Harvard University (Wasson 1972c); he sent a signed copy to the SOAS library, which I accessed during the course of research.

46. In the Vedic arena, notably endorsed by Falk (1989; 2002/3); see also Madhihassan (1987) and Qazilbash (1960); and in Zoroastrian ritual by, amongst others, Boyce (2012). Falk maintains (1989:79) that, "there is nothing shamanistic or visionary in early Vedic or in old Iranian texts". However, see Jurewicz (2010:177–182) for references in the *Ṛgveda* to how *soma* exultation can induce sensations of flying, omniscience, immortality and the ability to discern truth from a lack of truth. "Somic exultation is presented as a state which breaks the rules and limits of everyday experience" (p. 182). *Soma* can make one hot (not just metaphorically) (p. 194), as do some forms of *tapas*, notably in the Tibetan practice of generating bodily/psychic heat (*gtum-mo*: see Govinda 1969:159–165). Elizarenakova (1996) cites several Vedic passages in support of the 'visionary' nature of *soma*, which can provide visions of light and the sense of flying. Thompson (2003, 2006. 2016) does not propose an Ur-plant as *soma*, but similarly argues—*contra* Falk—that the experience of Vedic ritualists appears to be visionary or psychedelic.

47. See Nyberg (1997) for a survey of various ephedra species. He notes (p. 396) that the ephedra species with the highest ephedrine content is *Ephedra equistina*, which grows mainly in mountainous regions.

48. The term 'ephedrine' was coined for an extract from ephedra in the early 1920s by K. K. Chen, who produced a stimulant for medical use (Snyder 1986:131).

49. Various species of ephedra grow in Nepal (Rajbhandari 2001:53–54), Sikkim (Burman 2003:68), Kumaun district, Uttaranchal (Pranavananda 1983:148) and the Khyber Pass region of Afghanistan (Madhihassan 1987:10); it is used medicinally in all these regions. See Nyberg (1997) for details of species of ephedra native to places relatively far from the early Vedic heartland of Punjab.

Chinese medicine (as *mā huāng*), but in no culture that uses it is there any kind of reverence for this plant.

In Vedic ritual the *soma* concoction is drunk every few hours, sometimes over the course of several days. However, stimulants have a distinct threshold, beyond which—as, for example, with espresso coffee—the effects become decidedly unpleasant. Furthermore, as with any stimulant, the consumer will experience a hangover after the effect of a significant dose of ephedrine has worn off. Vedic ritualists, by contrast, appear to be 'reborn' after a *soma* rite, rather than hungover. Nevertheless, this does not rule out the possibility that ephedra was an additive plant to the *soma/haoma* concoction.

Even though ephedrine is a stimulant and not a psychedelic, clinical evidence has revealed that chronic use of stimulants such as ephedrine, methylphenidate, methamphetamine and modafinil may also induce auditory and visual hallucinations; the prime cause being the disruption to the Default Mode Network (DMN),[50] which may be caused by not only psychedelic drugs but also by stimulants and various neurological disorders (Alderson-Day *et al.* 2016).[51] Chronic use of stimulants such as amphetamines or cocaine, being dopamine agonists, can also engender hallucinations, psychosis and paranoia (Hobson 2001:235; Snyder 1986:138–140). Hobson (2001:35) comments that, "Any drug that interferes with the synthesis, release, reception or enzymatic breakdown of serotonin, norepinephrine, or acetylcholine is potentially psychedelic, and potentially psychonoxious". However, having

50. See also Kent (2010:34) for his theory of how interruption to 'top-down' organization in the brain is disrupted by psychedelic agents; when modular functions of the brain are uncoupled from top-down coherence, they do not always disappear, they may spontaneously organize into more locally coherent configurations. However, the inhibition of top-down control—mediated primarily via the dorsolateral prefrontal cortex—is not the only mechanism implicated in psychedelic experience (Hobson 2001:234).

51. Steve Farmer kindly provided this reference and additional information on this point.

considered the wide range of non-ordinary states of consciousness that can be engendered by consuming many kinds of compounds, it would seem more likely that the plants used in ancient Vedic and Zoroastrian rites were tryptamines that could induce 'classic' mystical states, rather than merely hallucinations and strange, unpleasant experiences.

4. AYAHUASCA AND AYAHUASCA ANALOGUES

It is well known that at least two plants are currently usually used in South America for making ayahuasca, which is a potentially psychedelic/entheogenic concoction: one is a plant containing DMT (*N,N*-dimethyltryptamine), a powerful psychedelic[52] with similar but not identical potential effects to those of the other 'classic' tryptamine alkaloids, namely LSD and psilocybin; the second main ingredient is a plant containing a monoamine-oxidase inhibitor (MAOI). The evidence indicates that this formula may have been in use in South America for around three or four hundred years (Torres 2018:43–49).

In South America the DMT is usually provided by the *chacruna/chakrona* plant (*Psychotria viridis*), while the *Banisteriopsis caapi* vine provides the MAOIs in the form of harmine, harmaline and tertahydroharmine.[53] The consumption of an MAOI-containing plant[54] at the same time as a DMT-containing plant allows the absorption of orally consumed DMT, which otherwise would be rapidly dissolved by enzymes produced in the liver, rendering the DMT inactive.[55]

52. See Strassman (2001); St John (2015).

53. Another similar psychedelic concoction used in some regions of South America is *yagé*, which is usually made, primarily, from the *Banisteriopsis caapi* vine and another vine, *Diplopterys cabrerana* (known locally as *chaliponga*), which also contains DMT and 5-MeO-DMT. For the distribution of the use of various tryptamine-containing plants in South America, see Torres (2017:38).

54. The function of MAO inhibition was first discovered in 1958 (Ott 1994:39). See Snyder (1986:98–100) on how the enzyme MAO is responsible for the oxidative deamination of the neurotransmitters norepinephrine and serotonin.

55. In some communities the macerated *Banisteriopsis caapi* vine is consumed uncooked, mixed with water, but without an additional DMT-containing plant (Stafford 1977:262; Ott 1994:17;

Attention has also been drawn (Clark 2020) to the ritual practices of the ayahuasca-using Santo Daime church,[56] which have some substantial and interesting parallels with the Vedic rituals of Brahmans and the ritual practices of Zoroastrians. This indicates that the use of ayahuasca analogues would be entirely consistent with the performance of Vedic and Zoroastrian ritual.

Over sixty plants are now known to contain DMT (and sometimes also 5-MeO-DMT) in various amounts, while around seventy plants are known to have MAOI properties.[57] These lists of plants are being almost annually augmented. This means that numerous plant combinations, which are globally distributed, could potentially provide analogues of ayahuasca. However, not all MAOI/DMT plant combinations are equally efficacious, as some plants also contain toxins that would undermine the experience; work is on-going regarding the most efficacious combinations.[58] A further consideration, which will be explored in further detail below, is that in the traditional manufacture of ayahuasca in South America not only are plants containing DMT and MAOIs used, but many other plants are nearly always added to the concoction.

A part of the argument for *soma/haoma* being an ayahuasca analogue formula is that the evidence for *soma/haoma* comprising complex plant formulas is in plain view in the relevant texts. In the *Avesta* there

---

1996a:208; Beyer 2010:221). At least one group in Brazil uses cold-pressed extractions of *vinho da jurema* (*Mimosa hostilis/tenuiflora*), which contains DMT (Ott 1997b:9).

56. Founded in Rio Branco, Acre Province, in Brazil, around 1930. For an account of the Santo Daime church and its beliefs and practices, see Alverga (1999).

57. Ott (1994:73–75; 81–83) lists sixty-seven plants with MAO-inhibiting β-carbolines and sixty-two plants with one or more of nineteen entheogenic tryptamines; see also Smith (1977) for a list of plants containing DMT and other tryptamines.

58. See Palmer (2015:32–39) for reports of bio-assays with various species of acacia growing in Australia.

are references to "many *haoma*s",[59] while in the *Veda*s there are also references to several kinds of *soma*.[60] Other plants are revered in the *Veda*s alongside *soma*;[61] some of them could possibly be complementary MAOI plants.[62] Furthermore, in the Indian *materia medica* around twenty plants are called '*soma*'.[63] Some of these plants have never been properly analysed for psychoactive properties, while some are known to be psychoactive. A multiplicity of possible *soma* formulas would explain why so many plants are called '*soma*' or '*haoma*'. As noted previously, a rough, contemporary comparison could be made with the modern term 'psychedelic' (coined by Humphry Osmond in the mid-1950s), which refers to the effects of a drug rather than to any particular plant or substance.

---

59. Staal (2001:763) expressed surprise and puzzlement as to why there are "many *haoma*s" in the *Avesta*.

60. For example: *ṚV* 9.65.23, "(May the Somas) which are in Ārjīka, Kṛtva or in the middle of rivers (or homesteads), or among the five peoples (be beneficial to us)"; *ṚV* 10.94.3, "...Chewing the twig of the red (Soma) tree"; *ṚV* 10.89.5, "Soma is released from all woods even dry"; *ṚV* 10.977: *soma* is said to be in all plants/herbs (*sarvā oṣadhīḥ*) (trans. Kashyap).

61. See Clark (2020:135–146) for information on other possible plant candidates for the *soma* formula.

62. In the *Atharvaveda* (19.39.5–6, 8) *soma* is mentioned in connection with the *aśvattha* (peepal) tree and also the *kuṣṭha* plant, which is usually identified as either snow lotus or as wild ginger (*Costus speciosus*); I speculate that the ginger plant may instead be galangal/aromatic ginger (*Kaempferia galangal*), which is used in Asian cooking, grows in South Asia, and is rich in MAOIs (Noro *et al.* 1983; Toro and Thomas 2007:46). The *kuṣṭha* plant is revered in the highest terms in the *Atharvaveda* (5.4): it is from the hills and is a remedy (v. 1) against *takman* (which is probably leprosy); it is descended from the gods, as *soma*'s benign friend (v. 7); it is a powerful healing plant (v. 10); it comes from the snowy mountains. The gods won the *kuṣṭha* plant in the third heaven—at their seat, the *aśvattha*—and brought it in a golden ship (6.95); it is a flower of immortality (v. 2); it is the best of plants (19.39.4); it cures all maladies and stands by the side of *soma* (19.39.5–8) (trans. Kashyap).

63. See Srivastava (1966:812–816) for a list of around twenty plants called *soma, somalatā, sum, hom* and the like in Indian medical texts. For the use of these plants in medicine and their synonyms, see Nadkarni (1954; 1998). See Swamy (1976) for a list of 'substitute' *soma* plants mentioned in the *Brāhmaṇas*. For an overview and discussion of some of these plants, see Clark (2020:135–146).

5. COMPLEX PLANT FORMULAS

One of the issues pertinent to this inquiry is the difference in approach to plant medicines in both ancient and modern indigenous cultures, and by contrast in the approach of modern allopathic medicine.

In modern allopathic medicine, plants known to be used or effective in traditional cultures as remedies are usually analyzed and tested with the aim of isolating a particular molecule or chemical ingredient that is most effective in the treatment of a malady. The isolated ingredient, which is generally concentrated and more potent than in its plant form, is then marketed as a drug, which may be manufactured in combination with other isolated ingredients from other plants or with a synthetic chemical. One of the factors in the manufacture and sale of patented drugs is, of course, the financial gain that accrues; far more than would be derived from the sale of a natural plant remedy.

In contrast, in most traditional cultures effective medicinal plants are very often used in combination with other plants. In many traditional remedial formulas not only is the full spectrum of the chemical ingredients of the medicinal plant consumed but additionally the full spectrum of ingredients of other plants. Plant combinations may have a synergetic effect more potent than that derived from a single plant. For example, when the Prussian naturalist Robert Hermann Schomburgk was trying in 1937 to identify the plant used in South America for making the poison *curare*, applied to the darts of poison arrows, it was originally believed that the essential poison of *curare* derived from just one liana, *Strychnos toxifera*, and that the admixture plants used by natives to make the poison were redundant. This view subsequently proved to be incorrect: the additive plants have a synergetic effect, increasing the potency of the *curare* (Plotkin 1993:155–156). The great botanist and explorer Richard Evans Schultes would eventually identify and document more than seventy species of plants employed to make *curare* in the Amazon region (Plotkin *et al.* 2017:102).

In Āyurvedic medicine in South Asia it is apparent that for the treatment of most maladies, complex plant formulas are recommended.[64] The *Saṃhitās* (compendia) of Caraka and Suśruta and the *Āśtāṅgahṛdaya* (*Heart of Medicine*) by Vāgbhaṭa are the three foundational texts of Āyurveda.[65] If we peruse the many dozens of medical formulas provided by Caraka, Suśruta and Vāghbaṭa, it is readily apparent that for a host of medical issues remedies may comprise four or five or even up to thirty or more plants or their extracts. These remedies are used in formulas for oleation, fomentation, emesis, purgation and other treatments.[66]

64. See also Sobiecki (20018:177ff.) for the use of complex plant formulas used in *ubulawu* medicines for initiation in South Africa.

65. The earliest formulations of the texts of both Caraka and Suśruta date to the early centuries BCE; these medical texts attained, after additions, their current form in the early centuries CE. Vāghbaṭa probably lived around 600 CE (Wujastyk 1998:40, 105, 238).

66. As an example, in Caraka's chapter on purgatives (*Sūtrasthāna*, ch. IV), it is said (p. 82) that, "There are six hundred purgatives, six different parts of the plant useful for purgation, five varieties of drugs for the preparation of decoction, five different pharmaceutical processes, fifty important varieties of decoctions and five hundred decoctions" (trans. Sharma and Dash, 1976). Caraka similarly details several formulas comprising numerous plant combinations for the treatment of

6. THE USE OF AYAHUASCA ANALOGUES

It is impossible to know when humans first made use of plants that can be most easily comprehended today as analogues of ayahuasca. In the modern era, the scientific discovery of the chemistry of the entheogenic effects of the combination of DMT with an MAOI is attributed to the research of Holmstedt and Lindgren, which was published in 1967 (Ott 1995:49; 1996b; 1997b; 1999); but in 1955 William Burroughs had already alerted Richard Schultes to the importance of the importance of the combination of *Psychotria viridis* and the *Banisteriopsis caapi* vine, to produce the 'fireworks' of the *yagé* experience (Burroughs and Ginsberg 1971), which information Schultes presented at a conference in Los Angeles in 1967 (Lees 2016:108–112).[67] Nevertheless, apart from a few isolated reports, it was not until the 1980s that a significant body of research began to be published on ayahuasca analogues (sometimes referred to as 'anahuasca').[68]

---

parasites (*Vimānasthāna*, ch. VIII, pp. 205–206), and for enemas (*Vimānasthāna*, ch. VIII, pp. 286–291). Dozens of multiple-plant formulas—some of which also comprise powdered metals or shells or the urine or skin of various animals—are also detailed by Suśruta. For example, ten plants are combined in a paste in a formula for a purgative (*Cikitsa Sthānam*, vol. 2, ch. IV:293); another formula (p. 295) for a disturbed *vāta dośa* contains twenty-nine plants, which should be mixed with salt; eight different plants are listed in one of the formulas for treating blood disease; fourteen plants comprise a formula for a poultice (p. 300); another for a plaster (*pradeha*) contains thirteen plants; one treatment for internal piles uses nine plants (p. 324); urinary problems may be treated with various formulas, one comprising twenty-one plants, another comprising twenty-three plants (p. 329); one treatment for leprosy and other diseases contains twenty-four plants (p. 349); another for abscesses has twenty-seven plants; another treatment for skin disease contains twenty-four plants (p. 508); a combination of twenty-one plants may serve for an enema; an afflicted eye can be treated with a mixture of twenty-two plants (vol. 3, *Uttara Tantram*, ch. XI:42); a combination of twenty plants can be used to treat insanity (ch. LXI:390). Vāgbhaṭa largely synthesizes the information, remedies and medical techniques of Caraka and Suśruta.

67. See also St John (2015:20–34) for a comprehensive account of Burroughs' engagement with DMT.

68. Notable amongst publications that have contributed to a wider understanding of this

One of the consequences of the diffusion of this information, partly as a consequence of the widespread use of the internet since the 1990s, is a global trend—albeit conducted by a small number of people—to experiment with combinations of various kinds of tryptamines (such as psilocybin mushrooms or *Mimosa tenuiflora*, which contains DMT), with other plants (such as Syrian rue) which contain MAOIs. Samorini (2019a) has coined the term 'X-huasca' for these novel combinations.[69] Also, a number of researchers have focused their attention on the possible use of ayahuasca analogues in various cultures in the past. The evidence for the historical use of ayahuasca analogues provided in reports by researchers is in some instances more robust while other claims remain somewhat speculative for the moment.

Although numerous species of the acacia tree contain DMT,[70] Shanon's proposition (2008) that ayahuasca analogues were made in Biblical Old Testament times from *Peganum harmala* (containing the MAOIs harmine, hamaline and tetrahydroharmine) and DMT extracted from *Acacia nilotica* is almost certainly unfounded, until further evidence is forthcoming, as this species of acacia contains no DMT.[71]

---

phenomenon are those of McKenna *et al.* (1984a; 1984b); Gracie and Zarkov (1985); Ott (1994; 1996a; 1996b; 1997b; 1999), Rätsch (2005) [1998]:716–720; DeKorne *et al.* (2002) [2000], and Keeper of the Trout (2002 [1993–2001]; 2004a [1998–2001]; 2004b [1997]). See, particularly, Ott (1994).

69. Turner (1994:62–72) reports on the potentiating effect of rue with other psychedelics; Ott (1994:65) notes how β-carbolines can enhance the effects of peyote.

70. Voogelbreinder (2018) provides the DMT content of around sixty species of acacia.

71. There are reports that *Acacia nilotica* contains DMT: Sobiecki (2002:9), for example, cites Hutchings *et al.* (1996:122), who report *N,N*-dimethyltryptamine (DMT) in the leaves. However, no DMT has been recorded in this species in more recent phytochemical analyses: Auwal *et al.* (2013); Sawant *et al.* (2014). Voogelbreinder (2009:69) has a substantial, referenced entry on this point: earlier claims of DMT and 5-MeO-DMT in this plant are unfounded. Leaves, stem bark, roots and seeds have all tested negative for alkaloids. Similarly, Trout (2002:15) notes claims of DMT in this species, but references negative results in subsequent alkaloid tests; however, one test in 1996 (p. 120) revealed "faint traces" of 5-MeO-DMT. Rätsch (2005:909) does not include this variety of acacia in his list of around fifty kinds of psychoactive acacias.

Sadji's proposal (2018: 'The Acacia Tree, The Sacred Vine & The Midianites'), which echoes that of Shannon (above), maintains that at the time of the composition of the Old Testament of the Bible, ayahuasca analogues were concocted in north-east Arabia and at Midian (in the area of the Red Sea and Sinai) by Midianites and others. Extracts of certain species of acacia are said to have provided DMT, while *Peganum harmala* (Syrian/mountain rue), provided MAOIs. Intriguing as the theory might be, this supposition currently remains somewhat speculative; however, further research may elicit additional corroborating evidence.

Similar ayahuasca analogue claims have been made for ancient Egypt by Myers (2011) and Christie (2014), who refers to Myers. Both commentators propose that ayahuasca analogues were used in ancient Egypt; Myers (p. 162ff.) goes further, suggesting that this formula was used also by Gnostics. The 'Tree of Life', which is sometimes represented in Egyptian art (Baines 2013:80; Manniche 1999:65–66), is correctly identified by Myers and Christie as *Acacia nilotica*, which is claimed provided the DMT for ayahuasca analogues. However, as noted above, this species of acacia contains no DMT. Furthermore, neither ancient nor more modern (Coptic) Egyptian texts record entheogenic properties of this tree; though several practical and medicinal uses are reported, such as for skin disease (Manniche 1999:65–67).[72]

Chemical analysis was undertaken by Miller *et al.* (2019) of the contents of a ritual bundle in a leather bag containing the remains of plants, discovered in a rock shelter in the Sora River valley in the Lipez highlands of the Andes mountains in southwestern Bolivia, which was excavated in 2008 and 2010. The ritual bundle was estimated to be

72. Zulus in Africa also employ *Acacia nilotica* for a variety of medicinal purposes (Hutchings *et al.* 1996:122).

around a thousand years old. Tests revealed the presence of bufotenine, DMT, harmaline and cocaine; at least three different plants are implicated. (This is the largest archeological find so far of assembled psychoactive plants in a single situation.) Miller *et al.* (2019) suggest that the traces of bufotenine may derive from *Anadenanthera colubrina* (often called *vilca* or *cebil*) or *Anadenanthera peregrina* (called *yopo*), while the harmaline may derive from *Banisteriopsis caapi*, the vine usually used to make ayahuasca.[73] None of these plants nor the *coca* plant is native to the Bolivian highlands. Harmaline (an MAOI) and DMT are sufficient for concocting an ayahuasca analogue.

73. It is also possible that the harmaline may derive from other more proximate plant sources (personal communication from Giorgio Samorini, 18/08/2019).

7. MULTIPLE PLANT FORMULAS USED FOR AYAHUASCA

As mentioned previously, the main, contemporary formula for ayahuasca comprises the *Banisteriopsis caapi* vine (containing MAOIs) and the leaves of one of the species of the *Psychotria viridis* bush (usually known as *chacruna*), which provides DMT. However, the brew usually comprises numerous other additive plants. Torres (2018:39) observes that, "An investigation into the origins of *ayahuasca* reveals numerous beverages distributed throughout South America, each being distinct and varying according to plant availability, cultural predilections for ingestion and ritual requirements." Torres (pp. 43–49) maintains that although some tryptamine-containing plants have been in use in South America since 2000 BCE, there is no evidence for use of the *Banisteriopsis caapi* vine for making ayahuasca before the initial contact with Europeans, *c.*1550–1650. However, Torres notes the use in South America of fermented drinks with an admixture of the DMT-containing seeds of *Anadenanthera peregrine*; and in the mid and upper tributaries of the Orinoco, the simultaneous consumption of *Banisteriopsis caapi* and the DMT-containing *yopo* could be seen as ayahuasca analogues.

Shepard (2018:75) comments that before the 1960s the Matsigenka tribe of the Manu region of Peru did not use the DMT-containing *Psychotria* species (*chacruna*) as an admixture to *Banisteriopsis.* Instead, they boiled the vine until it attained a honey-like consistency; sometimes tobacco or other plants were added.[74] Millard (2018:83)

74. Although the use of ayahuasca is currently associated in Amazonia with religious and medical uses, Shepard notes that for the Matsigenka the main use is to improve hunting skills. It is also

similarly observes that several tribes, including the Tukano (from the north-western region of Amazonia, mostly in Colombia), consume preparations of the *Banisteriopsis* vine without the use of additives. Voogelbreinder (2009:60) also remarks that the ayahuasca beverage sometimes comprises only *Banisteriopsis caapi* and that the most common additive is tobacco, rather than a DMT-containing plant. However, the most common practice is to brew potions with one or several additives (Ott 1994:26). As noted above, although the *Banisteriopsis* vine is usually boiled in water in the process of manufacture, some groups consume cold-water infusions of this plant (Ott 1994:17).

These days, as in the use of complex-plant formulas of traditional medicine discussed above, numerous additive plants usually comprise the ayahuasca drink (Ott 1994:19). Luna (1984:141) lists thirty-three plants that are variously added in Peru to the *Banisteriopsis caapi* plus *Psychotria viridis* ayahuasca combination.[75] Ott (1994:27–30) similarly provides a list of around a hundred ayahuasca additive plants from thirty-five botanical families. Ott (1994:20–21; 2006:18–19) also discusses plants containing stimulants such as caffeine; a relative of the caffeine-containing *guaraná* plant and the *coca* plant are added by some groups to their ayahuasca formulas. It could have been similar in Asia, where ephedra stalks or other plants containing ephedrine could have been added as booster plants to the formula. Some additive plants used by certain groups in South America contain traces of mescaline, iboga or tryptamines (Ott 1994:23).

---

occasionally used in the context of war and 'black magic' by some South American tribes (Saés 2011:136; De Mori 2011:28; Singh 2020)). In ancient Vedic tradition, *soma* was also used in rites for sorcery based on the *Sāmaveda*. The *Ṣadviṃśa Brāhmaṇa* contains sorcery rites called *śyena* (falcon), *iṣu* (arrow), *saṃdaṃśa* (tongs), and *vajra* (mace/thunderbolt); see Parpola (2015:134ff.) for further details.

75. See also Fotiou (2017:58–60).

Commenting on the profusion of ayahuasca additive plants discovered by researchers, Ott (1994:20) remarks that:

> Even more mysterious were the numerous *ayahuasca* admixtures for which we have no chemical data whatsoever. I agree with the authors that this category of admixture plants hold great potential interest for western science, and I expect further research will show that some of these unknown plants are psychoactive, while others have more specific therapeutic effects.

I would suggest that this observation is also highly pertinent to the study of plants that are either associated with or called *soma/haoma* in Asia.

8. ENTHEOGENIC PLANT TREATMENTS AND FORMULAS IN ĀYURVEDA

The task of identifying which plants may have been used to manufacture the ayahuasca analogues proposed as *soma/haoma* in ancient Asia is complex. Firstly, translations of the names of plants from ancient texts, such as the *Veda*s, which date from around 1600–700 BCE, may be of the names of plants in Sanskrit or derived from vernacular languages, at a time when plant identification was far more imprecise than it is nowadays.[76] Secondly, further compounding the difficulty of accurate plant identifications, in the modern era plant-family and species identifications are continually being modified by botanists, sometimes resulting in varying, more recent identifications.

During research into the plants that could have been used for ayahuasca analogues in ancient Asia, the properties of several plants that feature in Zoroastrian and Brahmanical texts were explored. However, besides being, as mentioned previously, an ancient and central component (together with the ritual worship of sacred fire) of both Vedic and Zoroastrian rites, *soma* also appears in Āyurvedic texts. Suśruta (1963:530–538 [vol. 2, ch. XXIX]), in a frequently-cited passage, describes a treatment for rejuvenation using *soma*. *Soma* is equated with *amṛta* (immortality), which, as noted previously, is one of the chief synonyms of *soma* in the *Veda*s. Suśruta names twenty-

76. To give just one example of many similar, problematic identifications: the plant/tree known as *karañja* has more than a dozen different botanical identifications (Meulenbeld 1974:537).

four kinds of *soma* plants,[77] which have various epithets, habitats and potencies.

The Āyurvedic rejuvenation treatment requires that the patient first undergoes ritual and dietary purification, including the use of emetics. After drinking *soma* the patient should not be allowed to sleep and should pass the night supervised by friends in a secluded room. The patient will vomit after drinking *soma*, which will purge him of worms and other obnoxious matter accumulated in the body as a result of wrong diet or conduct. For the next seven days the patient should only drink milk; he will become very thin but the vital spark of life will be maintained by *soma*. Various ointments should be applied to the body throughout the treatment. After twenty-four hours the patient may start eating gruel, by now with a renewed body (including a beautiful face and body and revitalized hair, skin and teeth). After a month, for the next ten days, the patient gradually spends more and more time outside the treatment chamber, eventually resuming normal life, fully endowed with great power and beauty.

Some of the names of the *soma* plants that Suśruta lists are mentioned in the *Vedas*; several of them, such as *agniṣṭoma* and *candramaḥ*, are well-known Vedic epithets for *soma*. Interestingly, Suśruta states (p. 531) that the virtues and methods of using them are identical; that, essentially, the effects are the same. However, it is apparent that different kinds of *soma* plant are referred to. Suśruta mentions that those which trail on the ground or grow as small shrubs or in bushes should be consumed as they are;[78] juice is not extracted from these kinds, but juice is extracted from the kinds called *aṃśumān* and *candramāḥ*, the latter

77. These names are: *aṃśumān, muñjavān, candramāḥ, rājaprabha, dūrvā soma, kanīyān, śvatākṣa, kanaka prabha, pratānvān, ṭāla vṛnta, karavira, aṃśavān, svaṃprabha, mahāsoma, garuḍāhṛta, gāyatra, traiṣṭubha, pāṃkta, jāgata, śāṃkara, agniṣṭoma, raivata, yathokta, udupati.*

78. The dose is said to be four *muśti*s (= 32 *tolā*s = *c.*350 gms.).

said to be the best kind of *soma.* Several varieties of *soma* are partially described: *aṃśumān* smells like ghee and has a bulb; *muñjavān* has leaves like those of a garlic plant; *candramāḥ* is golden-coloured and aquatic; *garuḍāhṛta* and *śvetākṣa* are yellowish, look like the cast-off skin of a snake, and hang from the boughs of trees. All other kinds are said (p. 537) to be marked with circular, motley-coloured rings, to have fifteen leaves which drop off with the waxing and waning of the moon, a creeper-like appearance,[79] and to secrete a milky juice.[80] Several kinds of habitats are mentioned, most of which are mountain ranges;[81] a few are aquatic.[82]

The discussion of *soma* plants by Suśruta is intriguing but puzzling. The claims made by Suśruta that teeth will regrow or that one can live for 10,000 years after a treatment are clearly unbelievable. However, could this be a confused, exaggerated report or an anecdotal memory of an ayahuasca-like treatment, after which the patient feels 'reborn'? Suśruta's names and descriptions of plants unfortunately provide virtually no clues as to the botanical identity of any of the plants used in this treatment for rejuvenation.

79. This description by Suśruta of *soma* plants is quite well known in India; it reappears in a biography/hagiography of Tapaswiji (Murthy 2003:35–37), a saint who is said to have lived for 165 years (1770–1955). Tapaswiji is reported to have met another saint living in a cave near Badarinath, who was 5,000 years old. This saint used to consume the juice, which is like milk, of the crushed leaves of the vine-like *soma-latā,* together with milk. Similar to the description by Suśruta of one of the plants, this creeper, of which there are said to be fifteen varieties, had red spots on the leaves. During the course of the lunar cycle, leaves appear on the plant one-by-one, until, on the full moon, there are fifteen leaves. The saint reports that consumption of this *soma* has allowed him to live for "thousands of years."

80. The leaves are said to sprout at the rate of one per day during the waxing moon of the 'bright half' of the lunar month, which fall off over the next fifteen 'dark' days of the lunar month. Suśruta also states that the bulb of the *soma* plant should be pricked to extrude a milky juice, which is to be consumed without being tasted.

81. Himālaya, Arvuda, Sahya, Mahendra, Malaya, Śrī Parvata, Devagiri, Devasaha, Pāripātra, Vindhya.

82. In Lake Devasunda; floating on the Indus river (*candramāḥ*); in 'little' Mānasa lake in Kashmir (*gāyatrī, traiṣṭubha, pāṃkta, jāgata, śaṃkara*).

More substantial information about *soma* plant formulas is contained in the Bower Manuscript, a sixth-century text from Kashmir, which is South Asia's earliest preserved medical text. In this text there are two complex plant formulas for *amṛta*, for use in a therapeutic context (Hoernle 2011:20n.64, 90, 106). One of the formulas is for *amṛta prāśa* (food) *ghī* (clarified butter), and the other is for *amṛta* oil.[83] Between them, the two formulas comprise around a hundred herbal ingredients, many of them of uncertain botanical classification.

Leonti and Casu (2014) examine the Bower Manuscript and observe that although the exhilarating effects of the *amṛta* concoctions are not described, the presence of DMT and MAOIs in several of the plants listed could potentially engender psychedelic/entheogenic experience, functioning as ayahuasca analogues. The formulas for *amṛta* are presented in the Bower Manuscript in a therapeutic/medical context, where it would seem that sub-entheogenic effects are sought, rather than an entheogenic effect from a higher dose. Leonti and Casu propose that these formulas in stronger doses were the basis for the *soma* of the *Veda*s.

From the formulas in the manuscript Leonti and Casu discuss six of the ingredient plants, all of which are native to South Asia and known to have psychoactive properties. These are (1) *Desmodium gangeticum (Fabaceae)*, (2) *Mucuna pruriens (Fabaceae)*, (3) *Nelumba nucifera (Nelumbonaceae)*, (4) *Sida rhombifolia, Sida spinosa* and *Sida cordifolia (Menispermaceae)*, (5) *Tabernaemontana divaricata (Apoyneae)*, and (6) *Tinosporia cordifolia (Menispermaceae).*

---

83. Hoernle (2011:90n.55) notes that the formula for *amṛta ghī* also appears in *Caraka Saṃhitā* (VI, 16, 1.22ff.); in Vāgbhaṭa's *Aṣṭāṅga Hṛdaya* (IV, 3, vv.93b–100) in a somewhat expanded form, and in contracted form in Vaṅgasena's *Saṃhitā* (XI, vv.38–43) and *Bhāva Prakāśa* (II.2). In the latter, minor ingredients are altered.

1. *Desmodium gangeticum* (Sanskrit *soma/śālaparṇī/śālapattrā*, Hindi *capakno*, sticky desmodium) is rich in both DMT and 5-MeO-DMT; it also has trace amounts of β-carboline (Shulgin and Shulgin 1997:208; Trout 2004b:9–13; Leonti and Casu 2014:378).[84]

2. *Mucuna pruriens* (Sanskrit *kappicacchu/ātmagupta*, Bengal velvet bean/cowhage) is similarly another plant that similarly contains, besides other alkaloids, both DMT and also, in trace amounts, 5-MeO-DMT, nicotine, serotonin, bufotenin, and β-carboline (Ghosal *et al.* 1971; Trout 2002:123). This plant also contains L-DOPA (L-3-4-dihydroxyphenylalanine), which is psychoactive and has a history of use in the treatment of Parkinson's disease (Lees 2016:23–27, 48–49).

3. *Nelumbo nucifera* (lotus plant) contains no tryptamines but is mildly psychoactive owing to the presence of nuciferene and nornuciferene, which act as mild sedatives. It has medicinal uses, particularly in China.[85]

4. All three of the *Sida* species (*S. rhombifolia*/arrowleaf sida, *S. spinosa*/prickly fanpetals, and *S. cordifolia*/flannel weed/country mallow) discussed by Leonti and Casu contain the stimulant ephedrine, besides other carboxylated tryptamines (Pramunick *et al.* 2015:130).

5. The fifth plant assessed by Leonti and Casu, *Tabernaemontana divaricata* (Sanskrit *nandīvṛkṣa/nata*; Hindi *candnī/tagar*; pinwheel flower/crape jasmine/East India rosebay) contains a substantial amount of ibogaine (Leonti and Casu 2014), a potentially powerful psychedelic.[86]

84. Another variety, *Desmodium barbatum*, which also contains β-carbolines, is used for epilepsy in Zimbabwe and as an anti-convulsant in Liberia (Sobiecki 2002:10).

85. See Clark (2020:108–110) for a detailed discussion of this plant; it has been proposed as *soma* by several commentators.

86. For the native use of iboga in the *bwiti* religion of Gabon/Camaroon, see Schultes, Hofmann and Rätsch (2001:112–115); Fernandez (1982:470ff.). For the chemistry and botany of ibogaine (the main active ingredient of the iboga plant), see Schultes and Hofmann (1980:235–239).

6. The sixth plant, *Tinospora cordifolia* (Sanskrit *guḍuci/madhuparṇi/soma/amṛta*, heart-leaved moonseed) contains jatorrhizine, berberine and plamatine, all of which, individually, act as MAOIs (both MAOI-A and MAOI-B).[87]

Taking into account the phytochemical profiles of the plants noted above, Leonti and Casu conclude that a psychoactive potion could be produced by making a concentrated juice of *Tinospora cordifolia*, which contains MAOIs (and which is called *soma* in the *materia medica* of India), and *Desmodium gangeticum*, which contains DMT (and which is also called *soma* in the *materia medica* of India). Leonti and Casu observe that the alkaloid content of *Tinospora cordifolia* and *Desmodium gangeticum* is considerable. The inclusion of any one of the *Sida* species would add a stimulant (namely ephedrine) dimension to the concoction. The addition of either ibogaine (in *Tabernaemontana divaricata*) or nuciferine (in *Nelumbo nucifera*) would also enhance the psychoactive effect of a concoction, but in different ways.

It is apparent that just the psychoactive effects of the plants analyzed above would be sufficient to act as ayahuasca analogues. This is without the further addition of the numerous plants in the formulas for *amṛta* in the Bower Manuscript for which few if any phytochemical profiles are currently available.

One of the ingredient plants in the *amṛta* formulas in the Bower Manuscript that is not discussed by Leonti and Casu is *kṣīravidārī/vidārī* (*Ipomoea digita*, a kind of morning glory), which is probably (but not certainly) a source of LSA.[88] The inclusion of this probably tryptamine-

87. For further details, see Clark (2020:141–146).

88. As noted previously (n.40), LSA (lysergic acid amide/ergine) can induce psychedelic effects. Some species of morning glory (particularly Pearly Gates and Heavenly Blue) have a substantial alkaloid content. See Schultes and Hofmann (1980:256–257) for variant botanical identifications. The seeds of this plant were used and revered historically by the Aztecs and Mayans of Mexico

containing plant in a *soma* formula would doubtless enhance effects.[89]

Among other plants included in the *amṛta* formulas is *kuśa/darbha* grass (*Desmostachya bipinnata*). The supremely 'holy' *kuśa/darbha* grass[90] features abundantly in both Buddhist[91] and Hindu rituals[92] and mythology.[93] *Kuśa* is occasionally mentioned in association with *soma*[94] and is praised in the highest terms in the *Atharvaveda.*[95] In the Brahmanical tradition there are many references to the numinous power of *soma.*[96] Deeg (1993:100ff.) maintains that in older Vedic literature *darbha* was used as intoxicant and that the effects of the plant resulted in it being referred to in the *Ṛgveda* (10.136) as *viṣa* (poison), as a consequence of it being used incorrectly. Although Deeg

and known as *ololiuqui.* Schultes identified the plant in the 1930s; Hofmann subsequently revealed the chemistry. *Ipomoea* species are still used in shamanic rituals in Mexico by Chontal, Mazatec and Zapotec Indians.

89. It is well known in Āyurveda as an aphrodisiac; see, for example, Vaṅgasena (ch. 78:p. 1114, v. 22). Various species of *Ipomoea* are also used in South Africa and Zimbabwe for psychedelic effects, divination, communication with ancestors, magical rituals, the treatment of madness and dream induction (Sobiecki 2002:8).

90. See Clark (2020:38–39n.140; 40n.150) for the botanical identification of *kuśa.*

91. See Beer (2003:21–23) for the mythology and use of *kuśa/dharba* grass in Buddhist rituals.

92. Gonda (1985:45) remarks that, "Occasionally the use of *kuśa* grass is prescribed almost to excess".

93. See Mani (1989:32) for the mythology of this grass in the *Purāṇa*s; see Pandey (1994:66, 100, 266–272) for its use in domestic Brahmanical rituals; see Clark (2020:149–154) for further general references.

94. *Atharvaveda* 11.6.15.

95. It has numinous power and can turn enemies away; it is of divine birth (*AV* 19.32.6–7); wearing an amulet made of *darbha* grass destroys rivals (*AV* 10.28.1); the power of *darbha* can make us luminous (*AV* 19.32.9); the healing remedies are *aśvattha* (the peepal tree), *darbha* and *soma* (8.7.20) (trans. Kashyap).

96. The *Kauṣītaki Brāhmaṇa* (8.8) appears to discuss mixing *soma* with *darbha* grass (though this passage may be referring to a 'magical' mixing rather than a real mixing of plants). The *Taittirīya Saṃhitā* (of the *Yajurveda*) (2.5.3.5) alludes similarly to a mixture of grass and *soma*; the *darbha*s are described (5.6.4.2–3) as, "ambrosia [the drink of immortality], the strength (*vīrya*) of the (earth)". Gonda (1982:62) comments that, "*dūrvā* grass is often used in lustrations and other auspicious rites, believed to cause happiness, prosperity and even to be akin to *soma*".

presents considerable evidence that *darbha* was considered to be an intoxicant or a drug, he does not explain how this common grass could have produced such a powerful effect. Perhaps the reason is that some species of *darbha* (or *kuśa*) may contain DMT and 5-MeO-DMT.

Darbha/kuśa grass (in the family of *Graminaceae/Gramineae/ Poaceae*) is a relative of *Phalaris* grass, some of the twenty or so varieties[97] of which contain (variously) DMT, 5-MeO-DMT and other alkaloids.[98] There is a growing body of discussion about extracting these chemicals from the plant (Clark 2020:152–153n.488); combined with an MAOI an ayahuasca analogue could be produced (Festi and Samorini 2004).[99]

Also in the list of plants in the *amṛta* formulas in the Bower Manuscript are *plakṣa* (*Ficus infectoria*, wavy-leaf/white fig tree), *udumbara* (*Ficus glomerata/racemosa*, Indian/cluster fig tree), *aśvattha* (*Ficus religiosa*, peepal/bodhi tree), and *nyagrodha/vaṭa* (*Ficus bengalensis/ benghalensis*, banyan tree).[100] None of these plants is currently known

97. There are nine species in the USA, four of them introduced from Europe (DeKorne *et al.* (2002:94).

98. DeKorne (2011:158, 171); Ott (1996a:246); Shulgin and Shulgin (1997:261, 418). For the alkaloid content of different varieties of *Phalaris*, its global distribution, and for the most comprehensive of bibliographies to date on these grasses, see Festi and Samorini (1993:265–289).

99. See DeKorne *et al.* (2002:85–123) for bioassays of Syrian rue plus extracts of *Phalaris* grass. *Kuśa* grass is still to be properly analysed for tryptamines. The author has made several attempts. Crowley (2014) observes that *Phalaris* grass may contain both tryptamines—including 5-MeO-DMT, which is orally active on its own according to Ott—and β-carbolines; he proposes that *Phalaris* grass was the grass known as *agrostis* to ancient Greeks and used to for psychedelic effects, though he is sceptical (p. 8) that the ancient Greeks knew of the potentiating effects of an MAOI. However, Syrian rue, the holy *moly*, was well known to the Greeks. Crowley nevertheless echoes the reservations of Festi and Samorini (1993) about the possible toxicity of *Phalaris* owing to the presence of gramine and hordenine in some varieties. I have argued (Clark 2020) that *kykeōn* was most probably, similarly to *soma/haoma*, an ayahuasca analogue.

100. *Nyagrodha, udumbara, aśvattha, plakṣa* and either *pārīśa* (*Thespesia populnea*) or *sirīśa* (*Albizzia lebbek*) or *vetasa* (*Calamus rotang*) are also said in the Bower Manuscript (Hoernle 2011:20n.64) to be the five trees with a milky sap. A north-American variety of the calamus plant (*Acorus calamus* L.) was prized by Native Americans for medicinal, ritualistic and dietary uses. It is mildly psychoactive; concentrated extracts can be used to manufacture the amphetamine

for any psychoactive property but very little work has been done to test for such properties.[101] All of these plants feature significantly as 'holy' plants[102] in the *Vedas*, *Purāṇas* and other South Asian religious texts and my hunch is that tests may reveal potential psychoactive properties. However, this supposition remains entirely speculative at the moment.

TMA-2 and MDA (Fester 2006:83–102, 132). *Acorus calamus* is used by Zulus for nervous disorders (Sobiecki 2002:5) and was one of the many ingredient plants in medieval witches' potions (Voogelbreinder 2009:58); see also Hatsis (2015); Ott (1995:45–46n.17) for plants used by witches.

101. Tests on *Ficus religiosa* (Singh and Goel 2009) have revealed significant levels of serotonin (5-HT) and consequent anti-convulsant properties, which could exist potentially useful to treat conditions such as epilepsy.

102. In the Hindu tradition there are five holy trees: peepal (*aśvattha*), banyan (*nyagrodha*), *gūlar* [Hindi] (Sanskrit: *udumbara*), *pākar* [Hindi] (Sanskrit: *plakṣa*), and mango; the most holy is the peepal (Pandey 1989:22). See Emeneau (1949) for references to fig trees in Sanskrit literature.

9. OTHER PLANTS POSSIBLY USED FOR *SOMA/HAOMA*

Another tree of interest in this regard, but not mentioned in the Bower Manuscript, is the *parṇa/palāśa* tree (*Butea frondosa/monosperma*, flame of the forest), which has a close mythological association with *soma*. In South Asia the myth of the theft or acquisition of *soma* has several variant forms (and also parallels in European and Middle-Eastern mythology). In the *Veda*s *soma* is said to have been brought to earth (or to Indra or to the gods) from either a hundred fortresses, a rock, a mountain top, or from heaven by either a falcon (*śyena*) or an eagle (*suparṇa*) bearing it/Him; or prised from hiding in nets of iron, or snatched from a cloud by lightning. In one version of the myth, *śyena* steals *soma* from Kṛśānu (the footless archer, its guardian), who hurls an arrow at *śyena*, causing a feather to fall to earth, which becomes the *parṇa* tree. As far as I am aware, no substantial, phytochemical tests have so far been undertaken on this plant to establish if it may potentially have psychoactive properties.

Is giant reed (*Arundo donax*) another plant that may possibly have been used in *soma/haoma* concoctions? Some varieties contain DMT and 5-MeO-DMT.[103] In the *Avesta* (*Y* 10.12, 17) *haoma* is said to be of

103. Some species of *Arundo donax*, which is widely distributed in India and Nepal, contain a range of alkaloids similar to those found in *Phalaris*, including bufotenin, DMT, 5-OH-DMT. 5-MeO-MMT, and 5-MeO-DMT (Festi and Samorini 1993:264; Trout 2002:27; Trout 2004c; Al-Snafi 2015:35). Anonymous (2005) has published a method for extracting DMT from *Phragmitis australis*, a common reed. He also claims that, in combination with an MAOI, *Arundo donax* can be potentiated to a psychedelic level when smoked. Ott (1996a:246) confirms the presence of DMT in these and other grasses; he also records (Ott 1994:73) the presence of MAOI β-carbolines in *A. donax*. In a report in the *Entheogen Review* (Winter 1992, DeKorne *et al.* 2002:126), entitled 'Sufi Ayahuasca…The Soma of the Aryans', the author states: "According to an acquaintance who was sworn to secrecy by a Sufi musician, *Peganum harmala* [Syrian rue] and the roots of

"many kinds" (Boyce 1975:158). The term *haoma* occurs frequently in the *Avesta* in the plural form. Boyce (2001:5) remarks that, "The ritual offering to the waters at the end of the *yasna* [ritual worship] was prepared from milk,[104] the leaves of one plant and the juice obtained from pounding the stems of another". Taillieu (2012) notes an indication that *haoma* was pressed together with a plant called *hadhānaēpata*,[105] which is a word of disputed meaning, and that when in a ritual *hadhānaēpata* is called for, "in the known Zoroastrian rite a pomegranate twig is used, but this must be a substitute for the original plant". Pomegranate has a long history of being divinized in the Mediterranean region and the Middle-East, since the time of the Sumerian empire, *c.*3000 BCE (Nigro and Spagnoli 2018), but is not psychoactive at all. In the *Avesta* there are several references to *hadhānaēpata*, nearly always in association with *haoma*, and propitiated with the same reverence.[106]

Flattery and Schwarz (1989:76ff.) do not accept the identification of *hadhānaēpata* with pomegranate. Although they do not propose an alternative botanical identification, they point out that although *haδāna* means 'with seeds' or 'seedy', it cannot be pomegranate because *haδānaēpātā* (sic) is said in the *Avesta* to be not only an intoxicant but also incense, which smells pleasant when burned; pomegranate cannot

Arundo donax were and are the source of a secret entheogen used in particular musical orders since before Islam influenced the Sufis." Samples of *Arundo donax* tested in India have the highest DMT content (Ghosal *et al.* 1969; Trout 2004c). Bio-assays and tests of various specimens of *Arundo donax* from the USA were mixed (DeKorne *et al.* 2002:126–131): some samples contained no DMT; others tested positive for DMT; others had alkaloids that caused nausea.

104. In descriptions of both Zoroastrian *haoma* and Vedic *soma* concoctions, milk is added to the pounded plant preparations. Milk fats may aid the absorption of psychoactive molecules; see Yasui-Furukori *et al.* (2002).

105. *Y* 68.1: "...let the Zaothra [priest] then attain for thee (for satisfaction), for it is thine with its Haoma, and its milk, and its Hadhānaēpata" (trans, Mills, *Zend-Avesta*).

106. *Y* 3.3: "And I desire to approach the Haoma-water, and the fresh milk with my praise, and the plant Hadhānaēpata" (trans. Mills, *Zend-Avesta*); similarly, *Y* 22.1; *Y* 52.9; *Y* 66.1; *Y* 68.1; and also *Visperad* 11.2.

be used for either purpose. *Haδānaēpātā* is a soft wood (*Vīvēvdād* 14.2–3), unlike pomegranate, which is a hard, close-grained wood that is useful for a slow-burning fire. *Haδānaēpātā* is left undefined and untranslated in the surviving Pahlavi textual tradition and has no surviving cognates in later languages; its meaning was probably confined to the priestly caste. Could *Haδānaēpātā* be *Arundo donax*? This plant has many seeds (like Pampas grass), is a soft wood, and as noted below, some species contain several tryptamines. That said, Festi and Samorini (1993) point out that *Arundo donax* also contains the toxin gramine (donaxine), which may seriously detract from the desired effect. Further work needs to be done to see how probable it was that *Arundo donax* could have been pressed for *haoma* rituals.

Julian Palmer has undertaken pioneering research on the plant *Phyllodium/Desmodium/Hedysarum pulchellum* (L.) Desv.[107] This plant is native to Asia and grows in South India, Bengal, Bangla Desh, Sri Lanka and the Himalayas (GBIF 2019 [1813]). The plant has a range of medical applications (Velmurugan *et al.* 2014). Interestingly, this *Desmodium* species contains both 5-MeO-DMT and MAOI β-carbolines;[108] it also causes vomiting. Prepared in the form of a simple tea or infusion, the alkaloid content in this plant is sufficient to produce an entheogenic, ayahuasca-like experience. Palmer believes that this plant may have been the *soma* plant. This seems to be highly plausible but, in my view, only to the extent that it was probably one of the possible additive plants. It is difficult to determine whether or not this variety of *Desmodium/Phyllodium* is in fact different from *śālaparṇī* (*Desmodium gangeticum*), which, as observed above, was a

107. Personal communications, May–June, 2019.

108. Ott (1994:73, 82) notes the presence of both β-carbolines and DMT in *Phyllodium pulchellum*, which has been demonstrated to produce MAO inhibition in rat brains (Cai *et al.* 2016).

known *soma* plant.[109] The website 'Flowers of India' classes *Desmodium pulchellum* as 'Snowy Desmodium' and *śālaparṇī*.[110]

109. Palmer reports around twenty varieties of *Desmodium* growing just in Laos.

110. Garg (2020): https://www.flowersofindia.net/catalog/slides/Showy%20Desmodium.html

10. *SOMA* IN TANTRAS

There appears to be some evidence of psychoactive, multi-plant *soma* formulas in *Tantra*s,[111] in which there is a vast repository of information that would need a great deal of time to explore fully; below is merely a minor, preliminary observation.

In the *Kulārṇavatantra*, usually dated to around the 14th century, in the 5th *ullāsa* (section/chapter), described in some detail is a method and formula for making *kuladravya* (clan substance). This concoction is called *gauḍī*—it is also referred to as *amṛta*—and is said (v. 20) enable the *sādhaka* (spiritual aspirant) to obtain the company of Śiva. The ingredients include white *Acacia arabica,*[112] *Eugenia jambolana,*[113] *Grislea tomentosa*[114] (or *Cocos nucifera*),[115] *Terminalia*

111. In many *Tantra*s such as, for example, the *Śāradātilaka Tantra*, Soma, as a deity, is often specified, alongside other deities—as in many *Purāṇa*s—as an object of veneration or as an element in ritual worship. This text is attributed to Śrīlakṣmaṇadeśikendra, who, calculating from a list of teachers mentioned (Avalon 1982:2), may have lived around 800–900 CE. The *soma* creeper is mentioned (*paṭala* 23, v. 42): performing *homa* with *soma* creepers mixed with milk, the worshiper (*upāsaka*) will attain perfection and become like the sun. He will attain a longer life, no longer afflicted by mental or physical disease. Similarly, in the *Kaulajñānanirṇaya*—a text attributed to Matsyendranātha and dated to the 11th century CE by P. C. Bagchi—*soma* is included (*paṭala* 24, v. 8) in a list of substances to be used for external *pūjā*, together with many kinds of flowers, resins from trees mixed with honey, meat, incense and *aguru*. *Agaru* is the resin produced by the deciduous tree *Aguilaria* (Agarwood/Eagle Wood) as a defence against mould; it is a stimulant and tonic in Āyurvedic medicine; agarwood is these days very rare and highly valued for its scent, worth up to $100,000 per kilo (Sheldrake 2020:33). No further information is provided on the precise nature of *soma*.

112. = *Vachellia nilotica*/gum arabic tree/thorny acacia.

113. Also used as an antidote to poisons in India (Rätsch 2005:484).

114. = *Woodfordia fruticosa*.

115. = coconut.

chebula,[116] *Solanum indicum,*[117] *Trikaṭu* (three bitter herbs: *Gingiber officinale, Piper longum* and *Piper nigrum*), and molasses. The potion (*kuladravya*), which appears to be cold-pressed, should be treated with great respect.[118] In the current state of knowledge, it is very difficult to assess the potential effect of this formula.

116. = black/chebulic myrobalan

117. = black nightshade.

118. "If one goes into the house of a Kulācārya, he should then, in order to be released from sin, devotedly request for nectar [*amṛta*] and in its absence drink just water. Saluting the vessel offered by the Kulācārya one should receive it with devotion, otherwise he will have to go to Hell. One who resorts to *kuladravya* without bathing, without devotion or out of greed, he, O Kuleśvarī, falls to poverty. One wearing a turban or tailored upper garment or who is naked, who has disheveled hair, who is in company of some other persons, uneasy or angry, should not drink the *kuladravya*" (11th *ullāsa* vv. 15–18 (trans. Rāy).

11. CURRENT *SOMA* USE IN BENGAL

A recent, highly pertinent discovery is that *soma* is still being manufactured and consumed in Bengal. Ian Baker (forthcoming)[119] reports on a *soma* cult that is currently still active in Tarapith, an ancient centre of Tantric practices in Bengal. A sect of both male and female Tāntrikas there worship Nīlkanṭh Tārā (Blue-throated Tārā), known to them also as Sarasvatī, in rites that entail the drinking of *soma.*

According to Baker's informant, only a few initiates know the formula for the *soma* preparation, which is preserved in a handwritten manuscript inherited from the informant's guru. *Soma* is said to have formerly been consumed by all the initiates of this sect, but that is not the case these days. The great *soma* elixir comprises sixty-four ingredients, which are combined with fermented rice and buried underground for a month. Prior to drinking *somras* (the juice [*ras*] of *soma*) the assembled *sādhak*s offer cannabis leaves to the lineage's gurus and then consume them.

This *soma* formula is composed of some non-psychoactive ingredients, including spices such as cardamon and curcumin (in turmeric), *śilājīt* (a resinous extrusion from Himalayan rocks), *gul* (a kind of molasses), *aśvagandhā* (*Withania somnifera*),[120] and rauwolfia (*Rauvolfia serpentina*), a plant that significantly reduces blood pressure. Also included in the formula is *Datura stramonium*, which

119. Ian Baker kindly provided me with a draft of his forthcoming article.

120. *Aśvagandhā* ('horse-smell') is also known as Indian ginseng; this plant is used widely in Āyurveda for several purposes, including aphrodisiac.

at anything more than minute doses is a toxic and potentially lethal hallucinogen. It is an ingredient known usually as *toé* in South America that is sometimes added to ayahuasca brews. Datura is also used in some Tantric Buddhist rituals and in initiatory rites by some African and South American groups (Clark 2020:104–105).

A key ingredient of the *soma* formula is said to be the fermented juice of a vine, *somalatā*, which has creamy, white flowers, numerous branches and no leaves (which is similar to one of the descriptions of a *soma* plant provided by Suśruta, referred to in Section 10). One of Baker's informants suggested that this plant is *Sarcostemma brevistigma*. However, as noted in Section 3, this plant is currently used in Vedic rites elsewhere in India but has no psychoactive properties; so, it seems that this botanical identification is uncertain. The juice of the *somalatā* vine was also said to assist the fermentation of the other ingredients to the *soma* concoction. After the month-long underground fermentation, the concoction is served in a ritual in intervals of an hour or an hour and a half, in nine to eleven small clay cups.

The *soma* ritual is performed over the course of an entire night in order to attain both bliss (*ānand*) and the renowned, transcendent, 'fourth' state (*turīya*) of trance,[121] in which lies the esoteric wisdom/insight (*gyān*) of Tantric practice. The initial effect of the concoction is dizziness, followed by visions, typically of the Goddess, of light, and sometimes of snake-like figures, as very often reported by *ayahuasceros* (Metzner 1999:46–186). Heat may arise in the body. Typical *kuṇḍalinī* effects occur. The *somras* engenders powerful visionary experiences, which, according to Baker's informant, are not even closely equalled by the effects of cannabis, which is sometimes prepared as a concoction

121. This state is unlike the other three mental states of waking, dreaming or sleeping (a scheme that dates back to the classical *Upaniṣads*).

to produce milder effects. *Soma* is said to assist the *sādhak* on the path to the supreme realization.

This fascinating report illustrates how the performance of *soma* rites persists in South Asia. Further information on the identity of the other ingredients of the sixty-four constituents of the *soma* concoction will hopefully provide further insights into the botanical knowledge of psychoactive plants in South Asia.

12. CONCLUSION

In this monograph there has been an attempt to demonstrate that *soma/haoma* was almost certainly never a single plant. As often in Āyurvedic prescriptions, and as in the indigenous folk medicine cultures of many traditional societies, and as in contemporary usage in Bengal, *soma/haoma* is a multiple-plant formula that would have differed over time and according to geography, depending on the availability of plants. The name of the formula, *soma/haoma*, referred to a concoction derived from the expressed juice of plants, which was sufficiently psychoactive to engender mystical experiences, which in subtle and complex ways likely influenced the grand historical trajectory of the pursuit of enlightenment and liberation from cultural habits of mind.

A great deal of work remains to be done on which plants may have been used and the synergetic effects of psychoactive plant combinations. However, there are sufficient references in the relevant texts, many of which remain to be explored, and in contemporary usage, to enable further forays into the botanical knowledge of ancient and modern Asia.

REFERENCES

Primary Sources

Avesta:

The Religious Books of the Parsees (from Professor Spiegel's German Translation of the Original Manuscripts, in three Volumes) (trans. Arthur Henry Bleeck) (2005) [1864]. Elibron/[Hertford: Muncherjee Hormusjee Cama].

Le Zend-Avesta (trans. James Darmesteter) (1960) [1892], vol. 1, *La Liturgie (Yasna et Vispérad)*; (1960) [1893], vol. 2, *La Loi (Vendidad), L'Épopée (Yashts), Le Livre de Prière (Khorda Avesta)*. Paris: Adrien Maisonneuve.

The Zend-Avesta, Part III: *The Yasna, Visparad, Âfrîgân, Gâhs, and Miscellaneous Fragments* (trans. L. H. Mills) (1887) (*Sacred Book of the East*, vol. XXXI, ed. F. Max Müller). Oxford: Clarenden Press.

Āyurveda:

Caraka (1976). *Agniveśa's Caraka Saṃhitā* (Text with English Translation & Critical Exposition Based on Cakrapāṇi Datta's Āyurveda Dīpika by Ram Karan Sharma and Vaidya Bhagwan Dash) (The Chowkamba Sanskrit Series, vol. XCIV), vols. 1–2. Varanasi: Chowkhamba Sanskrit Series Office.

Hoernle, A. F. Rudolph (2011) [1898–1912]. *The Bower Manuscript (Facsimile Leaves, Nagari Transcript, Romanised Transliteration and English Translation with Notes).* New Delhi: Aditya Prakashan [Calcutta: Superintendent Government Printing, India].

Suśruta (trans. and ed. Kaviraj Kunjalal Bhishagratna (1963). *Sushruta Samhitā (English Translation)*, vols. 1–3 (The Chowkhamba Sanskrit Studies, vol. XXX). Varanasi: The Chowkhamba Sanskrit Series Office.

Vāgbhaṭa (trans. Kanjiv Lochan) (2017) [2007]. *Aśṭāṅga Hṛdayam – Sūtra Sthāna (Text with English Translation, Notes and Appendix)* (The Mohandas Indological Series, vol. 12). New Delhi: Chaukhamba Publications.

Vaṅgasena (trans. and ed. Nirmal Saxena) (2004). *Vaṅgasena Saṃhitā (or Cikitsāsāra Saṃgraha). Text with English Translation, Notes, Historical Introduction, Comments, Index and Appendices*, vols. 1–2 (Chowkhamba Sanskrit Studies, vol. CXXV). Varanasi: Chowkhamba Sanskrit Series Office.

***Brāhmaṇas*:**

The Gopatha Brāhmaṇa of the Atharva Veda (eds. Rajendralāla Mitra and Harachandra Vidyābushaṇa) (2012) [1872] (Bibliotheca Indica, New Series, nos. 215 and 252). Forgotten Books/[Calcutta: Asiatic Society of Bengal].

The Pravargya Brāhmaṇa of the Taittirīya Āraṇyaka: An Ancient Commentary on the Pravargya Ritual (trans. and ed. Jan E. M. Houben) (1991). Delhi: Motilal Banarsidass.

Ṛgveda Brāhmaṇas: The Aitareya and Kauṣītaki Brāhmaṇas of the Rigveda (trans. Arthur Berriedale Keith) (1925) (Harvard Oriental Series, vol. 25). Cambridge, Massachusetts: Harvard University Press.

Śatapatha-Brāhmaṇa, according to the Mādhyandana school (parts I–IV) (trans. and ed. Julius Eggeling (1995) [1882–1900] (*Sacred Books of the East*, vols. 12, 26, 41, 43, 44, ed. F. Max Müller). Delhi: Motilal Banarsidass/[Oxford: Clarenden Press].

Taittirīya Brāhmaṇa: Paul-Émile Dumont (1951). 'The Special Kinds of Agnicayana (or Special Methods of Building the Fire Altar) according to the Kaṭhas in the Taittirīya-Brāhmaṇa'. *Proceedings of the American Philosophical Society*, vol. 95, no. 6, December 21, pp. 628–675.

***Hōm Yašt*:**

Josephson, Judith (1997). *The Pahlavi Translation Technique as Illustrated by* Hōm Yašt (Studia Iranica Upsaliensis 2). Uppsala, Sweden: Uppsala Universitetsbibliotek.

Pirart, Éric (2003), *L'éloge mazdéen de l'ivresse: Édition, traduction et commentaire du Hōm Stōd* (Collection KUBABA, Série Antiquité IV). Paris/Budapest/ Torino: L'Harmattan.

***Manusmṛti*:**

Patrick Olivelle (trans. and ed.) (2004). *The Law Codes of Manu.* Oxford/New York: Oxford University Press.

***Purāṇas*:**

Agni Purāṇa (trans. and eds. J. L. Shastri, G. P. Bhatt, and N. Gangadharan) (Complete Unabridged English Translation) (1999). Delhi: Motilal Banarsidass.

Bhāgavata Purāṇa [Śrīmad Bhāgavatam] (trans. and ed. A. C. Bhaktivedanta Swami Prabhupada), vols. 1–41 (1976). New York/Los Angeles/London/Bombay: The Bhaktivedanta Book Trust.

Liṅga Purāṇa (Parts I–II) (trans. and ed. J. L. Shastri and a Board of Scholars) (Ancient Indian Tradition and Mythology Series, vol. 5) (1998) [1951]. Delhi/Varanasi/Patna: Motilal Banarsidass.

Mārkaṇḍeya Purāṇa (trans. and ed. F. Eden Pargiter) (Bibliotheca Indica, New Series) (1904). Calcutta: The Asiatic Society of Bengal/Varanasi: S. B. Singh, Indological Book House.

Vāyu Purāṇa (Part II) (trans. and ed. G. V. Tagare) (Ancient Indian Tradition and Mythological Series) (1988). Delhi/Paris: Motilal Banarsidass/Unesco.

***Tantras*:**

Kaulajnana-nirnaya (of the school of Matsyendranatha) (trans. and ed. P. C. Bagchi and Michael Magee) (Tantra Granthamālā, no. 12) (1986). Varanasi: Prachya Prakashan.

Kulārṇava Tantra (trans. and ed. Rām Kumār Rāy) (Tantra Granthamālā no. 7) (1999). Varanasi: Prachya Prakashan.

Śāradā-Tilaka Tantram (trans. A Board of Scholars) (Sri Garib Das Oriental Series no. 82), 2nd revised edn. Delhi: Sri Satguru Publications.

——— (trans. and ed. Arthur Avalon) (1982) [1933] (Tantrik Text Series, vol. XVII). Delhi/Varanasi/Patna: Motilal Banarsidass.

***Vedas*:**

[Atharvaveda] Atharva Veda, vols. 1–6 (trans. and ed. R. L. Kashyap (2011–2012). Bangalore: Sri Aurobindo Kapāli Sāstri Institute of Vedic Culture (SAKSHI).

[Ṛgveda] Rig Veda Samhitā, vols. 1–12 (trans. and ed. R. L. Kashyap) (2007–2009). Bangalore: Sri Aurobindo Kapāli Sāstri Institute of Vedic Culture (SAKSHI).

[Sāmaveda] Sāma Veda, vols. 1–2 (trans. and ed. R. L. Kashyap (2008–2011). Bangalore: Sri Aurobindo Kapāli Sāstri Institute of Vedic Culture (SAKSHI).

[Yajurveda] Yajur Veda (Taittirīya Samhitā), vols. 1–4 (trans. and ed. R. L. Kashyap (2011). Bangalore: Sri Aurobindo Kapāli Sāstri Institute of Vedic Culture (SAKSHI).

***Viṣṇusmṛti*:**

The Institutes of Vishnu (trans. Julius Jolly) (1986) [1880] (*Sacred Books of the East*, vol. 7, ed. Max Müller). Delhi: Motilal Banarsidass.

***Yoga*:**

[Haṭhapradīpikā] Hatha Yoga Pradipika (trans. Brian Dana Akers). Woodstock, New York: YogaVidya.com.

[Khecarīvidyā] The Khecarīvidyā of Ādinātha: A critical edition and annotated translation of an early text of haṭhayoga. London/New York: Routledge.

Secondary Sources

Abaev, Vassilij Ivanovitch (trans. Jacques Verenc) (1975). 'Contribution à l'histoire des mots: 1. Vieil-iranien hauma- et le nom eurasien du houblon'. In *Mélanges linduistique offerts à Émile Benveniste*, pp. 1–3. Paris: Société de Linguistique de Paris.

Alderson-Day, Ben, Kelly Diederen, Charles Fernybough, Judith M. Ford, Guillermo Horga, Daniel S. Margulies, Simon McCarthy-Jones, Georg Northoff, James M. Shine, Jessica Turner, Vincent van de Ven, Remko van Lutterveld, Flavie Waters, and Renaud Jardi (2016). 'Auditory Hallucinations and the Brain's Resting-State Networks: Findings and Methodological Observations'. *Schizophrenia Bulletin*, vol. 42, no. 5, pp. 1120–1123.

Allegro, John M. (1973) [1970]. *The Sacred Mushroom and the Cross: A study of the nature and origins of Christianity within the fertility cults of the ancient Near East.* London: Abacus/Sphere Books.

Al-Snafi, Ali Esmail (2015). 'The Constituents and Biological Effects of *Arundo donax* – A Review'. *International Journal of Phytopharmacy Research*, vol. 6, issue 1, pp. 34–40.

Alverga, Alex Polari de (trans. Rosana Workman) (1999). *Forest of Visions: Ayahuasca, Amazonian Spirituality, and the Santo Daime Tradition.* Rochester, Vermont: Park Street Press.

Anonymous (2005). 'DMT from Phragmitis Australis, the common reed', pp. 1–7. Shaman Underground Publications (accessed 20/01/2020). https://archive.org/stream/DMTFromPhragmitesAustralis/DMT%20From%20Phragmites%20australis_djvu.txt

Antia, Kersey H. (2006). 'Were Achaemenians Zoroastrians? How do we Resolve this Question? A Zoroastrian Viewpoint'. In Antonio Panaiano & Andrea Piras (eds.), *Proceedings of the 5th Conference of the Societas Iranologica Europœa, held in Ravenna, 6–11 October 2003* (vol. 1, Ancient and Middle Iranian Studies), pp. 13–17. Milano: Mimesis.

Auwal, Mohammed Shaibu, Sanni Saka, Patrick Azubuike Onyeyili, 'Ismail Alhaji Mairiga, Abdullahi Shuaibu, Amina Ibrahim, Fatima Abba Lawan, Ahmad Bello Thaluvwa, and Abdulhamid Baba Njobdi (2013). 'Glycaemic Activity of the Aqueous Pod Extract of *Acacia Nilotica* (Fabaceae) in Normoglycemic and Alloxan Induced Diabetic Wistar Strain Albino Rats'. *Journal of Medical Science*, vol. 13 (8), 15th November, pp. 761–766.

Bache, Christopher M. (2019). *LSD and the Mind of the Universe: Diamonds from Heaven.* Rochester, Vermont: Park Street Press.

Bailey, H. W. (1984). 'Vedic *kṣúmpa* – and Connected Data'. In S. D. Joshi (ed.), *Amṛtadhārā: Professor R. N. Dandekar Felicitation Volume*, pp. 17–20. Delhi: Ajanta Publications (India).

Baines, John (2013). *High Culture and Experience in Ancient Egypt.* Sheffield, UK/Bristol CT: Equinox Publishing.

Baker, Ian (forthcoming). 'Nectar of the Blue Goddess: A Living Tradition of Soma Consumption in Tarapith, Bengal'. In Erika Dyck and Chris Elcock (eds.) *Global Histories of Psychedelics* (publisher TBA).

Baker, John R. (2009). 'Psychedelics, Culture, and Consciousness'. In Eli Franco and Dagmar Eigner (eds.), *Yogic Perception, Meditation and Altered States of Consciousness* (Philosophisch-Historische Klasse Sitzungsberichte, 794 Band), pp. 389–405. Wien: Verlag der Österreichischen Akademie der Wissenschaft.

Bartholomae, Christian (1904). *Altiranisches Wörtebuch.* Strassburg: Verlag von Karl J. Trübner.

Bedrosian, Robert (2000). 'Soma among the Armenians', pp. 1–18 (accessed 29/01/2020) https://archive.org/details/SomaAmongTheArmenians_661/mode/2up

Beer, Robert (2003). *The Handbook of Tibetan Buddhist Symbols.* Chicago/London: Serindia Publications Inc.

Beyer, Stephan V. (2010) [2009]. *Singing to the Plants: A Guide to Mestizo Shamanism in the Upper Amazon.* Albuquerque: University of New Mexico Press.

Bowman, Raymond A. (1970). *Aramaic Ritual Texts from Persepolis* (The University of Chicago Oriental Institute Publications, vol. XCI). Chicago/Illinois: University of Chicago Press.

Boyce, Mary (1975–1982). *A History of Zoroastrianism*, vols. 1–2. Leiden/Köln: E. J. Brill.

——— (2001) [1979]. *Zoroastrians: Their Religious Beliefs and Practices.* London/New York: Routledge.

——— (2012) [1998]. 'Haoma ii. The Rituals'. In *Encyclopædia Iranica* (eds. Ehsan Yarshater *et al.*), vol. XI, pp. 662–67. New York: Columbia University Press.

Brown, Jerry B., and Julie M. Brown (2016). *The Psychedelic Gospels: The Secret History of Hallucinogens in Christianity.* Rochester, Vermont/Toronto: Park Street Press.

Burman, J. J. Roy (2003). *Tribal Medicine: Traditional Practices and Changes in Sikkim.* New Delhi: Mittal Publications.

Burroughs, William S., and Allen Ginsberg (1971) [1963]. *The Yage Letters.* San Francisco: City Lights Books.

Cai L, C. Wang, X. K. Huo, P. P. Dong, B. J. Zhang, H. L. Zhang, S. S. Huang, B. Zhang, S. M. Yu, M. Zhong, X. C. Ma (2016). 'Effect of Alkaloids Isolated from Phyllodium pulchellum on Monoamine Levels and Monoamine oxidase in Rat Brain'. *Evidence-Based Complementary and Alternative Medicine*, vol. 2016, pp. 1–6. Article ID 6826175 https://doi.org/10.1155/2016/6826175 (accessed 23/01/2020).

Christie, Ben (2014). 'The Egyptians had their own version of Ayahuasca they called 'The Tree of Life'. https://www.collective-evolution.com/2014/05/31/the-tree-of-life-acacia-nilotica/ (accessed 8/09/2019).

Clark, Matthew (2015). 'Soma and Ayahuasca'. In Dave King, David Luke, Ben Sessa, Cameron Adams, and Aimée Tollan (eds.), *Neurotransmissions: Essays on Psychedelics from Breaking Convention*, pp. 149–160. London: Strange Attractor Press.

——— (2016). 'Religious Sects, Syncretism, and Claims of Antiquity: The Dashanami-Sannyasis and South Asian Sufis'. In Raziuddin Aquil and David L.Curley (eds.), *Literary and Religious Practices in Medieval and Early Modern India*, pp. 61–92. New Delhi: Manohar.

——— (2018a). 'Amṛta, the Nectar of Immortality: What is it?'. *Amrita*, Issue 4 (Autumn/Winter), pp. 91–97.

——— (2018b). *The History and Mythology of the Kumbh Melā.* Lulu.com.

——— (2019a). 'Soma'. In Knut A. Jacobsen *et al.* (eds.), *Brill's Encyclopedia of Hinduism Online.* Leiden/Boston: E. J. Brill. https://referenceworks.brillonline.com/entries/brill-s-encyclopedia-of-hinduism/soma-COM_1010070045.

——— (2019b). '*Soma* and *Haoma*: Ayahuasca Analogues from the Late Bronze Age'. *Journal of Psychedelic Studies,* vol. 3, issue 2 (Special Issue: 'Psychedelics in History and World Religions'), pp. 104–116.

——— (2019c). 'Ancient Ayahuasca Analogues from Central Asia: Soma, Haoma and Kykeōn'. In Nikki Wyrd, David Luke, Aimée Tollan, Cameron Adams and Dave King (eds.), *Psychedelicacies: More Food for Thought from Breaking Convention*, pp. 25–36. London: Strange Attractor Press.

——— (2020) [2017]. *The Tawny One: Soma, Haoma and Ayahuasca.* London: Aeon Books.

Clark, Walter Houston (1969). *Chemical Ecstasy: Psychedelic Drugs and Religion.* New York: Sheed and Ward.

Crowley, Mike (2016). *Secret Drugs of Buddhism: Psychedelic sacraments and the origins of the Vajrayāna.* Hayfork, California: Amrita Press.

Crowley, Morris (2014). 'Agrostis: Tryptamines in the Crucible of Civilization'. *The Nexian*, 4th April. http://the-nexian.me/home/knowledge/index.php?option=com_content&view=article&id=86:agrostis-tryptamines-in-the-crucible-of-civilization&catid=13:knowledge&Itemid=108

Dandekar, R. N. (1958–1962). *Śrautakośa (Based on the Śrautasūtras* [Part 1] *and Kalpasūtras* [Part 2] *belonging to the various Vedic Schools)* (English Section, vol. 1, parts 1 & 2). Poona: Vaidika Saṃśodhana Maṇḍala.

——— (1994). 'Soma is not Fly-Agaric'. In S. S. Bahukar and Sucheta Paranjpe (eds.), Śruti-cintāmaṇiḥ (Prof. C. G. Kashikar Felicitation Volume), pp. 21–28. Pune: Tilak Maharashtra Vidyapeeth.

Dannaway, Frederick (2009). 'Thunder Among the Pines: Defining a Pan-Asian Soma'. *Journal of Psychoactive Drugs*, vol. 4 (1), March, pp. 67–84.

Deeg, Max (1993). 'Shamanism in the Veda: The *Keśin*-Hymn (10.136), the Journey to Heaven of *Vasiṣṭha* (ṚV 7.88) and the *Mahāvrata*-Ritual. *Nagoya Studies in Indian Culture and Buddhism (Saṃbhāṣa)*, vol. 14, pp. 95–144. Nagoya: Department of Indian Philosophy, Nagoya.

DeKorne, Jim (2011) [1994]. *Psychedelic Shamanism: The Cultivation, Preparation and Shamanic Use of Psychotropic Plants*, 2nd edn. Berkeley: North Atlantic Books.

DeKorne, Jim, David Aardvark, and K. Trout (2002) [2000]. *Ayahuasca Analogues and Plant-Based Tryptamines (The Best of the Entheogen Review 1992–1999)* (ER Monograph Series, No. 1), 2nd edition. Sacrameto, California: The Entheogen Review.

Demiéville, Paul (1970). *Revue de* Wasson [1968]. *T'Oung Pao (Archives)*, pp. 298–302. Leiden: E. J. Brill.

De Mori, Bernd Brabec (2011). 'Tracing Hallucinations: Contributing to a Critical Ethnohistory of Ayahuasca Usage in the Peruvian Amazon'. In Beatriz Caiuby Labate and Henrik Jungaberie (eds.) *The Internationalization of Ayahuasca* (Intercultural Studies on Ritual, Play and Theatre, vol. 16), pp. 23–47. Zürick/Berlin: LIT Verlag.

Digby, Simon (1984). 'Qalandars and Related Groups: Elements of Social Deviance in the Religious Life of the Delhi Sultanate in the Thirteenth and Fourteenth Centuries'. In Yohanan Friedmann (ed.), *Islam in Asia* (vol. 1, South Asia), pp. 60–108, Jerusalem/Boulder, Colorado: The Magnes Press, The Hebrew University/Westview Press.

Di Maio, Paula (2013). 'Ethnobotanical Identification of Echinopsis Pachanoi in Himachal Pradesh. A New Candidate for the Soma Plant?' https://www.academia.edu/5399240/Ethnobotanical_study_identifies native_c actus_in_Asia_new_candidate_for_vedic_Soma_Plant (accessed 3/01/2020)

Dioscorides, Padanius (trans. Tess Anne Osbaldeston and R. P. A. Wood) (2000). *De Materia Medica.* Johannesburg: Ibidis.

Doniger, Wendy (1997) [1990]. 'Somatic Memories of R. Gordon Wasson'. In Thomas J. Riedlinger (ed.), *The Sacred Mushroom Seeker: Tributes to R. Gordon Wasson*, pp. 55–59. Rochester, Vermont: Park Street Press.

Elizarenakova, Tatiana (1996). 'The problem of Soma in the light of language and style in the Ṛgveda'. In B. Nalini *et al.* (eds.), *Langue, Style et Structure dans le Monde Indien.* pp. 13–31. Paris: Bibliothèque de l'École des Hautes Études.

Emeneau, M. B. (1949). 'The Strangling Figs in Sanskrit Literature'. *University of California Publications in Classical Philology*, vol. 13.10, pp. 345–370.

Entheology.org (2020). 'Argyreia nervosa – Hawaiian Baby Woodrose' http://www.entheology.org/edoto/anmviewer.asp?a=28&z=10 (accessed 3/01/2020)

Falk, Harry (1989). 'Soma I and II'. *Bulletin of the School of Oriental and African Studies,* vol. LII, part 1, pp. 77–90.

——— (2002/3). 'Decent Drugs for Decent People: Further Thoughts on the Nature of Soma'. *Orientalia Seucana*, vol. LI–LII, 2002–2003, pp. 141–155.

Fatur, Karsten (2019). 'Sagas of the Solanaceae: Speculative ethnobotanical perspectives on the Norse berserkers'. *Journal of Ethnopharmacology*, vol. 244 (112151), pp. 1–8.

Feeney, Kevin (2010). 'Revisiting Wasson's Soma: Exploring the effects of preparation on the chemistry of *Amanita muscaria*'. *Journal of Psychoactive Drugs*, vol. 42, issue 4, pp. 499–506.

Fernandez, James W. (1982). *Bwiti: An Ethnography of the Religious Imagination in Africa.* Princeton: Princeton university Press.

Fester, Uncle (2006). *Practical LSD Manufacture*, 3rd edn. Green Bay, WI: Festering Publications.

Festi, Francesca, and Giorgio Samorini (1993). 'Alcaloidi indolici psicoattivi nei generi *Phalaris* e *Arundo (Graminaceae)*: una rassegna. *Annali dei Musei Civici di Roverto*, vol. 9, pp. 239–287.

——— (2004). '"Ayahuasca-like" effects obtained with Italian plants'. In *Actas II, Congreso Internacional para el Estudio de los Estados Modificados de la Consciencia,* Llèida, octobre 3–7, 1994, pp. 62–71. Barcelona: Institudo de Prospectiva Antropológica.

Flattery, David Strophlet, and Martin Schwarz (1989). *Haoma and Harmaline: The Botanical Identity of the Indo-Iranian Hallucinogen "Soma" and its Legacy in Religion, Language and Middle-Eastern Folklore* (Near Eastern Studies, vol. 21). Berkeley/Los Angeles/London: University of California Press.

Fotiou, Evgenia (2017). 'Plant Use and Shamanic *Dietas* in contemporary *Ayahuasca* Shamanism in Peru'. In Ghillean Prance *et al.* (eds.), *Ethnopharmacologic Search for Psychoactive Drugs (50th Anniversary Symposium, June 6–8 2017)*, vol. 2, pp. 56–69. London/Santa Fe: Synergetic Press, Ltd.

Furst, Peter T. (1988) [1986]. *Mushrooms: Psychedelic Fungi (Encyclopedia of Psychoactive Drugs: Hallucinogens).* London: Burke Publishing Company Limited.

Garg, J. M. *Flowers of India.net* (accessed 20/01/2020). 'Snowy Desmodium'. https://www.flowersofindia.net/catalog/slides/Showy%20Desmodium.html

GBIF (Backbone Taxonomy) (2019) [1813]. '*Phyllodium pulchellum* (L.) Desv.'. [*Journal of Botanical Agriculture*, vol. 1: 124, t. 5, 1813, "*pulchrum*"] https://www.gbif.org/species/2948568 (accessed 4/6/2019).

Gershevitch, Ilya (1974). 'An Iranianist View of the Soma Controversy'. In Ph. Gignoux and A. Tafazzoli (eds.), *Mémorial de Jean Menasce*, pp. 45–75. Louvain: Imprimerie Orientaliste.

Ghosal, S., S. K. Dutta, A. K. Sanyal, and S. K. Bhattacharya (1969). 'Arundo Donax L. (Graminae), Phytochemical and Pharmacological Evaluation'. *Journal of Medical Chemistry*, vol. 12, p. 480.

Ghosal, S., S. Singh, and S. K. Bhattacharya (1971). 'Alkaloids of *Mucuna pruriens*: Chemistry and Pharmacology'. *Planta Medica*, vol. 19 (3), pp. 279–294.

Gonda, Jan (1982). *The Haviryajñāḥ Somāḥ: The Interrelations of the Vedic Solemn Sacrifices: Śāṅkhāyana Śrautasūtra 14, 1–3, Translation and Notes* (Verhandelingen der Mededelingen der Koninklijke Nederlandse Akademie van Wetenschapen, AFD. Letterkunde, Nieuwe Reeks, Deel 113). Amsterdam/Oxford/New York: North Holland Publishing Company.

——— (1985). *The Ritual Functions and Significance of Grasses in the Religion of the Veda.* Amsterdam/Oxford/New York: North-Holland Publishing Company.

Govinda, Lama Anagarika (1969) [1960]. *Foundations of Tibetan Mysticism: According to the Esoteric Teachings of the Great Mantra Oṃ Maṇi Padme Hūṃ.* London: Rider & Company.

Gracie and Zarkov (1985). 'Three Beta-Carboline Containing Plants as Potentiators of DMT and Other Indole Psychedelics, pp. 1–7. (Reprint based on the text of *Notes from the Underground: A "Gracie and Zarkof" Reader*, vol. II, no. 7), as archived at: https://erowid.org/plants/syrian_rue/syrian_rue_info1_bklt.pdf (accessed 15/11/2019)

——— (1991) [1985]. *Notes from Underground: A "Gracie and Zarkov" Reader*, vol. II. Gracie and Zarkov Productions.

Griffiths, Roland R., W. A. Richards, U. McCann, and R. Jesse (2006). 'Psilocybin can occasion mystical-type experiences having substantial and sustained personal meaning and spiritual experience'. *Psychopharmacology*, vol. 187, pp. 268–283.

Griffiths, Roland R., M. W. Johnson, W. A. Richards, B. D. Richards, U. McCann, and R. Jesse (2011). 'Psilocybin occasioned mystical-type experiences: Immediate and persistent dose-related effects'. *Psychopharmacology*, vol. 218 (4), December, pp. 649–655.

Griffiths, Roland R., Ethan S. Hurwitz, Alan K. Davis, Matthew W. Johnson, and Robert Jesse (2019). 'Survey of subjective "God encounter experiences": Comparisons among naturally occurring experiences and those occasioned by the classic psychedelics psilocybin, LSD, ayahuasca, or DMT'. *PLoS One*, vol. 14, issue 4, April 23, e0214377, pp. 1–26.

Gupta, Shakti M. (2013). *Plant Myths and Traditions in India.* New Delhi: Munshiram Manoharlal Pvt. Ltd.

Hajicek-Dobberstein, Scott (1995). 'Soma siddhas and alchemical enlightenment: psychedelic mushrooms in Buddhist tradition'. *Journal of Ethnopharmacology*, vol. 48, pp. 99–108.

Hanegraaf, Wouter J. (2014) [2013]. 'Entheogenic Esotericism'. In Egil Asprem and Kennet Granholm (eds.), *Contemporary Esotericism (Gnostica: Texts and Interpretations)*, pp. 392–409. Abingdon, Oxon/New York: Routledge.

Hatsis, Thomas (2015). *The Witches' Ointment: The Secret History of Psychedelic Magic.* Rochester, Vermont/Toronto: Park Street Press.

——— (2016). 'Born of a Version: Parthenogenesis and the Holy Mushroom'. In Robert Dickins (ed.), *Psychedelic Press*, vol. XVII, pp. 21–39. London: Psychedelic Press.

Heinrich, Clark (1995). *Strange Fruit: Alchemy, Religion and Magical Foods. A Speculative History.* London: Bloomsbury Publishing.

——— (2014). 'Heaven and Hell'. In J. Harold Ellens (ed.), *Seeking the Sacred with Psychoactive Substances: Chemical Paths to Spirituality and to God*, vol. 1, pp. 291–297. Santa Barbara/Denver/Oxford: Praeger.

Hendricks, Peter S. (2018). 'Awe: a putative mechanism underlying the effects of classic psychedelic-assisted psychotherapy'. *International Review of Psychiatry*, vol. 30(4), pp. 1–12.

Herodotus (trans. and intro. Aubrey de Sélincourt) (1968) [1954]. *The Histories.* Harmondsworth, Middlesex: Penguin Books.

Hobson, J. Allan (2001). *The Dream Drugstore: Chemically Altered States of Consciousness.* Cambridge, Massachusetts/London, UK: MIT Press.

Hood Jr., Ralph W. (2014). 'Chemically Facilitated Mysticism and the Question of Veridicality'. In J. Harold Ellens (ed.), *Seeking the Sacred with Psychoactive Substances: Chemical Paths to Spirituality and to God*, vol. 2, pp. 179–199. Santa Barbara/Denver/Oxford: Praeger.

Horgan, John (2004). *Rational Mysticism: Spirituality Meets Science in the Search for Enlightenment.* Boston/New York: Mariner Books/Houghton Mifflin Company.

Houben, Jan E. M. (2003). 'The Soma-Haoma problem: Introductory overview and observations on the discussion'. *Electronic Journal of Vedic Studies [EJVS]*, vol. 9, Issue 1a (May 4).

Housten, Robert, and Jean Masters (2000) [1966]. *The Varieties of Psychedelic Experience (The Classic Guide to the Effects of LSD on the Psyche).* Rochester, Vermont: Park Street Press.

Hulin, Michel (2014) [1993]. *La mystigue sauvage: Aux antipodes de l'esprit.* Paris: Quadrige/Presses Universitaires de France.

Hutchings, Anne, Alan Haxton Scott, Gillian Lewis, and Anthony Cunningham (1996). *Zulu Medicinal Plants: An Inventory.* Pietermaritzburg: University of Natal Press.

Irvin, Jan, and Andrew Rutajit (2009) [2005]. *Astrotheology and Shamanism: Christianity's Pagan Roots (A Revolutionary Interpretation of the Evidence)*, 2nd edn. BookSurge.

Jay, Mike (1999). *Blue Tide: The Search for Soma.* Brooklyn, New York: Automedia.

Jurewicz, Joanna (2010). *Fire and Cognition in the* Ṛgveda. Warsaw: Dom Wydawniczy Elipsa.

Kane, Pandurang Vaman (1977–1997) [1930–1962]. *History of Dharmaśāstra*, vols. 1–5 (Government Oriental Series, Class B, no. 6), 3rd edn. Poona: Bhandarkar Oriental Research Institute.

Karamustafa, Ahmet T. (2006) [1994]. *God's Unruly Friends: Dervish Groups in the Islamic Middle Period 1200–1550.* Oxford: Oneworld Publications.

Kent, James L. (2010). *Psychedelic Information Theory: Shamanism in the Age of Reason.* Seattle, WA: PIT Press/Supermassive LLC.

Klapp, Edward (2013). 'Raven's Bread and Other Manifestations of Fly Agaric in Classical and Biblical Literature'. In John A. Rush (ed.), *Entheogens and the Development of Culture: The Anthropology and Neurobiology of Ecstatic* Experience, pp. 333–342. Berkeley, California: South Atlantic Books.

Knipe, David M. (2015). *Vedic Voices: Intimate Narratives of a Living Andhra Tradition.* Oxford/New York: Oxford University Press.

Koryakova, Ludmila, and Andrej Epimachov (2014) [2007]. *The Urals and Western Siberia in the Bronze and Iron Ages.* New York: Cambridge University Press.

Kuiper, Franciscus Bernados Jacobus (1984). 'Was the *putika* a Mushroom?' In S. D. Joshi (ed.), *Amṛtadhāra: Professor R. N. Dandekar Felicitation Volume*, pp. 219–227. Delhi: Ajanta Publications (India).

Lees, A. J. (2016). *Mentored by a Madman: The William Burroughs Experiment.* London: Notting Hill Editions.

Leprechaun (2008). 'Cheap Sweet Sufiuasca New World Style: Arundo donax & Passion Flower (Passiflora Incarnata)'. (accessed 13/01/2021) https://erowid.org/experiences/exp.php?ID=75834

Letcher, Andy (2007). *Shroom: A Cultural History of the Magic Mushroom.* London: Faber and Faber.

Levitt, Stephan Hillyer (2011). 'New considerations regarding the identity of Vedic *sóma* as the mushroom fly agaric'. *Studia Orientalia*, vol. 111, pp. 105–18.

Leonti, Marco, and Laura Casu (2014). 'Soma, food of the immortals according to the Bower Manuscript (Kashmir, 6th century AD). *Journal of Ethnopharmacology*, vol. 155, June, pp. 373–386.

Long, J. Bruce (1976). 'Life out of Death: A Structural Analysis of the Myth of the 'Churning of the Ocean of Milk'. In Bardwell L. Smith (ed.), *Hinduism: New Essays in the History of Religions* (Studies in the History of Religions, Supplement to *Numen*, vol. XXXIII), pp. 171–207. Leiden: E. J. Brill.

Luna, Luis Eduardo (1984). 'The Concept of Plants as Teachers among four Mestizo Shamans of Iquitos, Northeastern Perú'. *The Journal of Ethnopharmacology*, vol. 11(2), July, pp. 135–156.

Macdonnell, A. A. (1995) [1898]. *Vedic Mythology.* Delhi: Motilal Banarsidass.

Madhihassan, S. (1987). *The History and Natural History of Soma as Ephedra.* Islamabad: Pakistan Science Foundation.

Maillart-Garg, Meena, and Michael Winkelman (2019). 'The "Kamasutra" temples of India. A case for the encoding of psychedelically induced spirituality'. *Journal of Psychedelic Studies*, vol. 3, issue 2 (Special Issue: 'Psychedelics in History and World Religions'), pp. 81–101.

Malandra, William M. (trans. and ed.) (1983). *An Introduction to Ancient Iranian Religion: Readings from the Avesta and Achaemenid Inscriptions.* Minneapolis: University of Minnesota Press.

Mani, Vettam (1989) [1975]. *Purāṇic Encyclopedia.* Delhi: Motilal Banarsidass.

Manniche, Lise (1999) [1989]. *An Ancient Egyptian Herbal.* London: British Museum Press.

McEvilley, Thomas C. (2002). *The Shape of Ancient Thought: Comparative Studies in Greek and Indian Philosophies.* New York: Allworth Press.

McKenna, Dennis K., G. H. N. Towers, and F. Abbott (1984a). 'Monoamine oxidase inhibitors in South American hallucinogenic plants: Tryptamine and b-carboline constituents of *Ayahuasca*'. *Journal of Ethnobotany*, vol. 10, Issue 2 (April), pp. 195–223.

——— (1984b). 'Monoamine oxidase inhibitors in South American hallucinogenic plants part 2: Constituents of orally-active Myristicaceous hallucinogens'. *Journal of Ethnobotany*, vol. 12, Issue 2 (November), pp. 179–211.

McKenna, Terence (1992) [1984]. *Food of the Gods*. London: Rider.

Meulenbeld, G. Jan (1974). *The Mādhavavidāna and its Chief Commentary, Chapters 1–10* (Introduction, Translation and Notes). Leiden: E. J. Brill.

Metzner, Ralph |(ed.) (1999). *Ayahuasca: Human Consciousness and the Spirits of Nature.* New York: Thunder's Mouth Press.

Millard, Dale (2018). 'Broad Spectrum Roles of Harmine in *Ayahuasca*'. In Ghillean Prance *et al.* (eds.), *Ethnopharmacologic Search for Psychoactive Drugs (50th Anniversary Symposium, June 6–8 2017),* vol. 2, pp. 70–81. London/ Santa Fe: Synergetic Press, Ltd.

Miller, Melanie J, Juan Albarracin-Jordan, Christine Moore, and José M. Capriles (2019). 'Chemical evidence for the use of multiple psychotropic plants in a 1,000-year-old ritual bundle from South America'. *Proceedings of the National Academy of Sciences of the United States of America*, May 6, pp.1–33.

Modi, Jivanji Jamshedi (1922). *The Religious Ceremonies and Customs of the Parsis.* Mazagaon, Bombay: British India Press.

Müller-Ebeling, Claudia, Christian Rätsch, and Surendra Bahadur Shahi (2002). *Shamanism and Tantra in the Himalayas*. Rochester, Vermont: Park Street Press.

Murthy, T. S. Anantha (2003) [1968]. *Tapaswiji: Sreeman Tapaswiji Maharaj, Saint who lived for 165 years: A Biography*, 3rd edn. Bangalore: Sri Vishnu Ashram Trust Publications.

Myers, Luke A. (2011). *Gnostic Visions: Uncovering the Greatest Secret of the Ancient World.* Bloomington: iUniverse.

Nadkarni, K. M. (1954) [1908]. *Indian Materia Medica*, vols. 1–2, 3rd edn. Bombay/Panvel: Popular Book Depot/Dhootapapeshwar Prakashan Ltd.

——— (1998) [1910]. *Indian Plants and Drugs with their Medical Properties and Uses.* Delhi: Asiatic Publishing House.

Naranjo, Claudio (1973). *The Healing Journey: New Approaches to Consciousness.* New York: Ballantyne Books.

Navet, Éric (1988). 'Les Ojibway et l'amanite tue-mouche (*Amanita muscaria*). Pour une ethnomycologie des indiens d'Amérique du Nord'. *Journal de la Société des américanistes*, vol. 74, pp. 163–180.

Nigro, Lorenzo, and Federica Spagnoli (2018). 'Pomegranate (*Punica granatulum* L.) from Motya and its deepest oriental roots'. *Vicino Oriente*, vol. XXII, pp. 49–90. (Accessed 20/01/2020) http://www.journalvo.it/Publicazioni/VO%20XXII/VO_XXII_PDF_Autori/VO_XXII_049-090_Nigro-Spagnoli.pdf

Noro, Tadataka, Toshio Miyase, Masanori Kuroynage, Akira Ueno, and Sego Fukushima (1983) 'Monoamine Oxidase Inhibitor from the Rhizome of *Kaempferia galanga*'. *Chemical and Pharmaceutical Bulletin*, vol. 31, no. 8, pp. 2708–2711.

Nyberg, Harri (1997). 'The problem of the Aryans and the Soma'. In George Erdosy (ed.), *The Indo-Aryans of Ancient South Asia: Language, Material Culture and Ethnicity*, pp. 382–406. New Delhi: Munshiram Manoharlal.

O'Flaherty, Wendy Doniger (1969) [1968]. 'The Post-Vedic History of the Soma Plant'. In Wasson, pp. 95–147.

Osto, Douglas (2019). *Altered States: Buddhism and Psychedelic Spirituality in America.* New York/Chichester (UK). Columbia University Press.

Ott, Jonathan (1994). *Ayahuasca Analogues: Pangæn Entheogens.* Kennewick, WA: Natural Products Co.

——— (1995). *The Age of Entheogens & The Angels' Dictionary.* Kennewick, WA: Natural Products Co.

——— (1996a) [1993]. *Pharmacotheon: Entheogenic Drugs, their Plant Sources and History*, 2nd edn. Kennewick, WA: Natural Products Co.

——— (1996b). 'Pharmahuasca: On Phenethylamines and Potentiation'. *Newsletter of the Multidisciplinary Association for Psychedelic Studies [MAPS]*, vol. 6, no. 3, Summer, pp. 32–34.

——— (1997a). *Pharmacophilia or the Natural Paradises.* Kennewick, WA: Natural Products Co.

——— (1997b). 'Pharmahuasca, Anahuasca and Vinho da Jurema: Human Pharmacology of Oral DMT plus Harmine'. (Originally published in *Yearbook of Ethnomedicine 1997–98*). https://pdfs.semanticscholar.org/9f95/8be0924e28f2a2c25e13f7dceb03fc12aa78.pdf

——— (1998). 'The Post-Wasson History of the *Soma* Plant'. *Eleusis*, n.s., no. 1, pp. 9–37.

——— (1999). 'Pharmahuasca: Human pharmacology of oral DMT plus harmine'. *Journal of Psychedelic Drugs*, vol. 31, issue 2, April–June, pp. 171–177.

——— (2006). *Análogos de la Ayahuasca: Enteógenos Pangeicos*. Madrid: Ediciones Amargord.

Padhy, Sachidananda, and Santosh Kumar Dash (1997). 'Mushrooms as Prohibited Food in *Manusmṛti vis-à-vis Amanita Muscaria* as Vedic Soma Plant'. *Ethnobotany,* vol. 9, p. 129.

Palmer, Julian (2015). *Articulations: On the Utilisation and Meaning of Psychedelics*, 3rd edn. Anastomosis Books.

Pandey, Brahma Prakash (1989). *Sacred Plants of India.* New Delhi: Shree Publishing House.

Pandey, Rajbali (1994) [1969]. *Hindu Saṃskāras: Socio-Religious Study of the Hindu Sacraments.* Motilal Banarsidass Publishers Private Limited.

Parpola, Asko (2015). *The Roots of Hinduism: The Early Aryans and the Indus Civilization.* Oxford/New York: Oxford University Press.

Passie, Torsten (2019). *The Science of Microdosing Psychedelics.* London: Psychedelic Press.

Pendell, Dale (2010) [2002]. *Pharmako Dynamis: Stimulating Plants, Potions and Herbcraft.* Berkeley, California: North Atlantic Books.

Perrine, Daniel M. (1996). *The Chemistry of Mind-Altering Drugs: History, Pharmacology, and Cultural Context.* Washington, DC: American Chemical Society.

Piper, Alan (2019). 'Burāq depicted as *Amanita muscaria* in a 15th-century Timurid illuminated manuscript? *Journal of Psychedelic Studies,* vol. 3, issue 2, pp. 133–141.

Pliny (trans. W. H. S. Jones) (1961). *Natural History*, Books 20–23, 24–27 (vols. VI and VII, Loeb Classical Library). Cambridge, Massachusetts/London: Harvard University Press/William Heinemann.

Plotkin, Mark J. (1993). *Tales of a Shaman's Apprentice: An Ethnobotanist Searches for New Medicines in the Amazonian Rain Forest.* Harmondsworth, Middlesex, UK: Penguin Books.

Plotkin, Mark J., Brian Hettler, and Wade Davis (2017). '*Viva* Schultes – A Retrospective'. In Ghillean Prance *et al.* (eds.), *Ethnopharmacologic Search for Psychoactive Drugs (50th Anniversary Symposium, June 6–8 2017)*, vol. 2, pp. 95–119. London/Santa Fe: Synergetic Press Ltd.

Pramunick, D. D., G. G. Maiti, and A. Srivastava (2015). 'Micromorphological study of 'BALA' plant (*Sida cordifolia* L., Malvaceae) with special reference to its propagation technique'. *Journal of Medicinal Plant Studies*, vol. 3(4), pp.127–131.

Pranavananda, Swami (1983) [1949]. *Kailās-Mānasarovar*, 2nd edn. New Delhi: Swami Pranavananda.

Puharich, Andrija (1959). *The Sacred Mushroom: Key to the Door of Eternity.* Garden City, New York: Doubleday and Co.

Qazilbash, N. A. (1960). 'Ephedra of the Rigveda'. *The Pharmaceutical Journal*, vol. 26, November, pp. 497–501.

Rajbhandari, Keshab R. (2001). *Ethnobotany of Nepal.* Katmandu: Ethnobotanical Society of Nepal.

Rätsch, Christian (trans. John R. Baker) (2005) [1998, in German]. *The Encyclopedia of Psychoactive Plants: Ethnopharmacology and its Applications.* Rochester, Vermont: Park Street Press.

Rawala, G. S., R. Rawala, and M. P. Sharma (2002). 'Medicinally important agarics in Himalaya'. In S. S. Samant, U. Dhar, and M. S. Paini (eds.), *Himalayan Medicinal Plants: Potential and Prospects*, pp. 33–43. Nainital, India: Gyanodaya Prakashan.

Robinson, Trevor (1968). *The Biochemistry of Alkaloids (Molecular Biology, Biochemistry and Biophysics 3).* New York: Springer-Verlag New York Ltd.

Rojas-Aréchiga, Mariana, and Joel Flores (2016). 'An Overview of Cacti and the Controversial Peyote'. In Beatriz Caiuby Labate and Clancy Cavnar (eds.), *Peyote: History, Tradition, Politics, and Conservation*, pp. 21–42. Santa Barbara, California/Denver, Colorado: Praeger.

Ruck, Carl A. (2006). *Sacred Mushrooms of the Goddess and the Secrets of Eleusis.* Berkeley: Ronin Publishing, Inc.

Ruck, Carl A., Mark A. Hoffman, and José Alfredo Gonzáles Celdrán (2011). *Mushrooms, Myth & Mithras: The Drug Cult that Civilized Europe.* San Francisco: City Lights Books.

Rush, John A. (2011). *The Mushroom in Christian Art: The Identity of Jesus in the Development of Christianity*. Berkeley, California: North Atlantic Books.

Saar, Meret (1991). 'Ethnomycological data from Siberia and north-east Asia on the effect of *Amanita muscaria*'. *Journal of Ethnopharmacology*, vol. 341, issue 2, pp. 157–173.

Sadovski, Velizar (2018). 'Vedic and Avestan Parallels from Ritual Liturgies and Liturgical Practices 1'. In Lucien Beek, Alwin Kloekhorst, Gus Kroonen, Michaël Peyrot, and Tijmen Pronk (eds.), *Farnah: Indo-Iranian and Indo-European Studies in Honour of Sasha Lubotsky*, pp. 307–326. Ann Arbor/ New York: Beech Stave Press.

Saés, Oscar Calavier (2011). 'A Vine Network'. In Beatriz Caiuby Labate and Henrik Jungaberie (eds.) *The Internationalization of Ayahuasca* (Intercultural Studies on Ritual, Play and Theatre, vol. 16), pp. 131–144. Zürick/Berlin: LIT Verlag.

Sajdi, Rami (2018). 'Desert Land'. http://www.acacialand.com (accessed 3/08/2019).

Samorini, Giorgio (trans. Tami Calliope) (2002). *Animals and Psychedelics: The Natural World and the Instinct to Alter Consciousness*. Rochester, Vermont: Park Street Press.

——— (2017). 'Bibliografia su Soma e Haoma'/'General bibliography on Soma and Haoma'. www.samorini.it

——— (2018). *Archeologia delle piante inebrianti.* Tricase, LE, Italy: Youcanprint Self-Publishing.

——— (2019a).'Peganum Harmala, the "Ayahuasca" of North Africa and Eurasia'. https://kahpi.net/peganum-harmala-ayahuasca/ (accessed 15/08/2019).

——— (2019b). *Piante psicoattive: Studi etnobotanici.* Lecce, Italy: Youcanprint

Sawant, R. S., A. G. Godghate, S. A. Sankpal, S. A. Walaki, and S. S. Kankanwadi (2014). 'Phytochemical Analysis of Bark of *Acacia Nilotica*'. *Asian Journal of Plant Science and Research (Pelagia Research Library)*, vol. 4(2), pp. 22–24.

Schroder, Tom (2014). *Acid Test: LSD, Ecstasy, and the Power to Heal.* New York: Penguin/Blue Rider Press.

Schroeder, Robert F., and Gastón Guzmán (1981). 'A new psychotropic fungus in Nepal'. *Mycotaxon*, vol. 13(2), July–September, pp. 346–348.

Schultes, Richard Evans, and Albert Hofmann (1980). *The Botany and Chemistry of Hallucinogens.* Springfield, Illinois: Charles C. Thomas.

Schultes, Richard Evans, Albert Hofmann, and Christian Rätsch (2001) [1992]. *Plants of the Gods: Their Sacred, Healing and Hallucinogenic Powers*, 2nd edn. Rochester, Vermont: Healing Arts Press.

Schwarz, Martin (2006). 'On Haoma, and its Liturgy in the Gathas'. In Antonio Panaino and Andrea Piras (eds.), *Proceedings of the 5th Conference of the Societas Iranologica Europæa (held in Ravenna, 6–11 October 2003)* (vol. 1, Ancient & Middle Iranian Studies), pp. 215–224. Milano: Mimesis.

Seaford, Richard (2004). *Money and the Early Greek Mind: Homer, Philosophy, Tragedy.* Cambridge University Press.

Shanon, Benny (2008). 'Biblical Entheogens: A Speculative Hypothesis'. *Time and Mind: The Journal of Archaeology, Consciousness and Culture,* vol. 1, Issue 1, pp. 51–74.

Sheldrake, Merlin (2020). *Entangled Life: How Fungi Make our Worlds, Change our Minds, and Shape our Futures.* London: The Bodley Head.

Shepard, Glenn H. (2018). 'Spirit Bodies, Plant Teachers and Messenger Molecules in Amazonan Shamanism'. In Ghillean Prance *et al.* (eds.), *Ethnopharmacologic Search for Psychoactive Drugs (50th Anniversary Symposium, June 6–8 2017),* vol. 2, pp. 70–81. London/Santa Fe: Synergetic Press, Ltd.

Shulgin, Alexander, and Ann Shulgin (1997). *TiKHAL: The Continuation.* Berkeley: Transform Press.

——— (2000) [1989]. *PiKHAL: A Chemical Love Story.* Berkeley: Transform Press.

Siegal, Ronald K. (2005) [1989]. *Intoxication: The Universal Drive for Mind-Altering Substances.* Rochester, Vermont: Park Street Press.

Singh, Damanpreet, and Rajesh Kumar Goel (2099). 'Anticonvulsant effect of *Ficus religiosa*: Role of serotonergic pathways'. *Journal of Ethnopharmacology*, vol. 123, pp. 33–334.

Singh, Manvir (2020). 'Psychedelics weren't as common in ancient cultures as we think'. *Vice (Drugs)*, 10.12.2020. Vice Media Group. https://www.vice.com/en/article/4adngq/psychedelic-drug-use-in-ancient-indigenous-cultures

Smith, Frederick M. (2001). 'The Recent History of Vedic Ritual in Maharashtra'. In Klaus Kartttunen and Petteri Koskikallio (eds.), *Vidyārṇavadanum. Essays in Honour of Asko Parpola. Studia Orientalia*, vol. 94, pp. 443–453.

Smith, Huston (1972). 'Wasson's Soma: A review article'. *Journal of the American Academy of Religions*, vol. 40(4), pp. 480–499.

Smith, Terence A. (1977). 'Review: Tryptamine and Related Compounds in Plants'. *Phytochemistry*, vol. 16, pp. 171–175.

Snyder, Solomon H. (1986). *Drugs and the Brain.* New York: Scientific American Library.

Sobiecki, Jean-Francois (2002). 'A Preliminary Inventory of Plants used for Psychoactive Purposes in Southern African Healing Traditions'. *Transactions of The Royal Society of South Africa*, vol. 57(1 & 2), pp. 1–24.

——— (2018). 'Psychoactive Initiation Plant Medicines: Their Role in the Healing and Learning Process of South African and Upper Amazonian Traditional Healers'. In Ghillean Prance *et al.* (eds.), *Ethnopharmacologic Search for Psychoactive Drugs (50th Anniversary Symposium, June 6–8 2017),* vol. 2, pp. 175–180. London/Santa Fe: Synergetic Press, Ltd.

Srivastava, J. G. (1966). 'The Soma Plant'. *Quarterly Journal of Crude Drug Research*, vol. 10, no. 3, pp. 811–816.

Staal, Frits (2001). 'How a Psychoactive Substance Became a Ritual: The Case of Soma'. *Social Research*, vol. 68.3, pp. 745–778.

Stafford, Peter (1977). *Psychedelics Encyclopedia.* Berkeley, CA: And/Or Press.

Strassman, Rick (2001). *DMT: The Spirit Molecule.* Rochester, Vermont: Park Street Press.

Stuhrman, Rainer (1985). 'Worum handelt es sich beim Soma. *Indo-Iranian Journal*, vol. 28, pp. 85–93.

——— (2006) 'Capturing Light in the Ṛgveda: Soma seen botanically, pharmacologically, and in the eyes of the Kavis'. *Electronic Journal of Vedic Studies [EJVS]*, vol. 13, issue 1 (April), pp. 1–93.

St John, Graham (2015). *Mystery School in Hyperspace: A Cultural History of DMT.* Berkeley, California: Evolver Editions.

Stolaroff, Myron J. (1994). *Thanatos to Eros: Thirty-Five Years of Psychedelic Exploration.* Berlin: Verlag für Wissenschaft und Bildung (VWB).

——— (2004) [1997]. *The Secret Chief Revealed.* Sarasota, Florida: Multidisciplinary Association for Psychedelic Studies (MAPS).

Swamy, B. G. L. (1976). 'Sources for a History of Plant Sciences in India, II: The *Ṛg Vedic Soma* Plant'. *Indian Journal of History of Science*, vol. 11, no. 1, May, pp. 11–12.

Taillieu, Dieter (2012) [1998]. 'Haoma i. Botany'. In *Encyclopædia Iranica*, vol. XI, fasc. 6, pp. 659–662. http://www.iranicaonline.org/articles/haoma-i (accessed 20/012020)

Thompson, George (2003). 'Soma and Ecstasy in the Ṛgveda'. *Electronic Journal of Vedic Studies*, vol. 9, issue 1e (May 6), article 5, pp. 1–13.

——— (2006). 'On the Nāmarūpa of Soma'. *Nāmarūpa*, issue 5, Fall, pp. 65–69.

——— (2016). 'A Brief Anthology of Hymns in the *Ṛgveda* Having to Do with *Soma* (and Shamanism)'. In George Thompson and Richard K. Payne (eds.), *On Meaning and Mantras: Essays in Honor of Frits Staal*, pp. 557–577. Moraga, California: Institute of Buddhist Studies/BDK America, Inc.

Torres, Constantino Manuel (2018). 'From Beer to Tobacco: A Probable Prehistory of *Ayahuasca* and *Yagé*'. In Ghillean Prance *et al.* (eds.), *Ethnopharmacologic Search for Psychoactive Drugs (50th Anniversary Symposium, June 6–8 2017),* vol. 2, pp. 36–69. London/Santa Fe: Synergetic Press, Ltd.

Toro, Gianluca, and Benjamin Thomas (2007). *Drugs of the Dreaming, Oneirogens:* Salvia divinorum *and other Dream-Enhancing Plants.* Rochester, Vermont: Park Street Press.

Tortel, Christiane (2009). *L'Ascète et le Bouffon:* qalandars, *vrais ou faux renonçants en islam, ou l'Orient indianisé.* France: Actes Sud.

Trout, Keeper of the, *et al.* (2002) [1993–2001]. *Trout's Notes on Some Simple Tryptamines: A brief overview and resource compendium* (Trout's Notes #FS-X7, Version 4-2002). Mydriatic Productions/Better Days Publishing.

——— (2004a) [1998–2001] *A-5: Ayahuasca: alkaloids, plants & analogs*, 2nd edn. [1st edn.: *Trout's Notes on Ayahuasca & Ayahuasca Alkaloids*]. https://erowid.org/library/books_online/ayahuasca_apa/ (accessed 9/12/2019).

——— (2004b) [1997]. 'Trout's Notes on the Genus *Desmodium* (Chemistry, Ethnomedicine, Pharmacology, Synonyms and Miscellany), Trout's notes #D-2 (3-2002). Mydriatic Productions/Better Days Publishing.

——— (2004c). *Trout's Notes: Tryptamine Content of Arundo donax.* https://erowid.org/plants/arundo_donax/arundo_donax_info1.shtml (accessed 20/01/2020).

Turner, D. M. (1994). *The Essential Psychedelic Guide.* San Francisco: Panther Books.

Velmurugan, G., S. P. Anand, and A. Doss. (2014). '*Phyllodium Pulchellum*: A Potential Medicinal Plant – A Review'. *International Review of Pharmacy Review & Research*, vol. 4, issue 4, pp. 202–206.

Voogelbreinder, Snu (2009). *Garden of Eden: The Shamanic Use of Psychoactive Flora and Fauna, and the Study of Consciousness.* (Self-published).

——— (2018). 'Psychoactive Australian Acacia Species and Their Alkaloids' In Ghillian Prance *et al.* (eds.), *Ethnopharmacologic Search for Psychoactive Drugs, 2017 (50th Anniversary Symposium, June 6–8),* vol. II, pp. 181–201.

Wasson, R. Gordon (1969) [1968]. *Soma: Divine Mushroom of Immortality.* New York, NY: Harcourt Brace Jovanovich, Inc.

——— (1971). 'The Soma of the Rig Veda. What Was It?' *Journal of the American Oriental Society*, vol. 91, no. 2 (April–June), pp. 169–187.

——— (1972a). 'The Divine Mushroom of Immortality'. In Peter Furst (ed.), *Flesh of the Gods: The Ritual Use of Hallucinogens*, pp. 185–200. New York/ Washington: Praeger Publishers.

——— (1972b). 'What Was the Soma of the Aryans?'. In Peter Furst (ed.), *Flesh of the Gods: The Ritual Use of Hallucinogens*, pp. 201–213. New York/ Washington: Praeger Publishers.

——— (1972c). *Soma and the Fly-Agaric: Mr. Wasson's Rejoinder to Professor Brough.* Cambridge, Mass.: Botanical Museum of Harvard University.

Wasson, R. Gordon, Stella Kramrisch, Jonathan Ott, and Carl A. P. Ruck (1986). *Persephone's Quest: Entheogens and the Origins of Religion.* New Haven/ London: Yale University Press.

Watkins, Calvert (1978). 'Let Us Now Praise Famous Grains'. *Proceedings from the American Philosophical Society*, vol. 122, no. 1, pp. 9–17.

Winkelman, Michael (2014). 'Evolutionary Views of Entheogenic Consciousness'. In J. Harold Ellens (ed.), *Seeking the Sacred with Psychoactive Substances: Chemical Paths to Spirituality and to God*, vol. 1, pp. 341–364. Santa Barbara/Denver/Oxford: Praeger.

Wohlberg, Joseph (1990). 'Haoma-Soma in the World of Ancient Greece'. *The Journal of Psychedelic Drugs*, vol. 2, issue 3 (July–Sept), pp. 333–342.

Wujastyk, Dominik (1998). *The Roots of Āyurveda: Selections from Sanskrit Medical Writings.* New Delhi/London/New York: Penguin Books.

Yasui-Furukori, N, T. Kondo, T. Takahata, K. Mihara, S. Ono, S. Kaneko, and T. Tateishi (2002). 'Effect of dietary fat content in meals on pharmacokinetics of quazepam'. *Journal of Clinical Pharmacology*, vol. 42 (12), pp. 1335–1340.

Zaehner, R. C. (1972) [1969]. *Hindu and Muslim Mysticism.* Schocken Books: New York.

Zvelebil, Kamil V. (1996). *The Siddha Quest for Immortality.* Oxford: Mandrake of Oxford.

Psychedelic Press
Independent Book Publisher

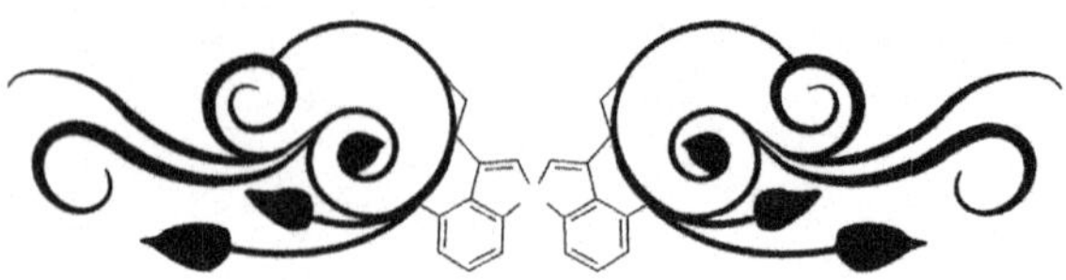

Printed in Great Britain
by Amazon

18587389R00048